Open Road's Best Of
THE FRENCH RIVIERA
& PROVENCE

Andy Herbach

OPEN ROAD GUIDES
Uncluttered
To the Point
Easy

OPEN ROAD PUBLISHING

Open Road's travel guides are designed to cut to the chase. You don't need a huge travel encyclopedia – you need a selective guide to steer you right. If you're going on vacation for a few weeks or less, our guides bring you the best of any destination for the amount of time you really have for your trip!

Open Road – the guide you need for the trip you want!

3rd Edition

OPEN ROAD PUBLISHING
www.openroadguides.com

Text Copyright © 2016 by Andy Herbach
- All Rights Reserved -
ISBN 13: 978-1-59360-218-5
Library of Congress Control No. 2015918261

About the Author
Andy Herbach is the author of several guides published by Open Road. He is the author of the Eating & Drinking series of menu translators and restaurant guides including *Eating & Drinking in Paris*, *Eating & Drinking in Italy*, and *Eating & Drinking in Spain & Portugal*. He is also the co-author of the Wining & Dining series of restaurants and wine bars, including *Wining & Dining in Paris* and *Wining & Dining in Italy*. Andy is also the author of *Open Road's Best of Paris*. Andy is a lawyer and resides in Palm Springs, California.

Acknowledgments
Special thanks to Jonathan Stein at Open Road Publishing. This book was edited in part by Marian Modesta Olson. Karl Raaum contributed to this book.

For photo credits and acknowledgments, turn to page 200.

Contents

Maps

1. Introduction

On the **French Riviera**, you'll discover pastel-colored villas with red tile roofs looking down on the turquoise waters of the Mediterranean Sea.

Some come to **Provence** for the savory cuisine and wonderful wines, while others visit quiet villages to get away from it all. There are also some of the world's best-preserved Roman ruins to see, and elegant seaside resorts where you can bask on sun-drenched beaches. You'll be dazzled by fields of lavender, yellow sunflowers and bright red poppies under brilliant blue skies.

Whatever your reasons to visit, there's truly something for everyone on the French Riviera and in Provence. Wherever you go, you'll create colorful memories.

You'll have more than 100 plac-es of interest at your fingertips (from colorful Old Nice to the Papal Palace in Avignon to the wineries in Châteauneuf-du-Pape), with insider tips on ca-fés, restaurants, hotels, shops, outdoor markets, and where to sample great wines.

This guide covers all the infor-mation you need to plan your trip without burdening you with a long list of options that simply aren't worth your precious vaca-tion time. Just take off and en-joy–you've got a great adventure ahead!

2. Overview

Get ready to explore Roman ruins, eat fantastic food, enjoy bustling outdoor markets, or just sit in the sun and sip a glass of chilled wine.

Nice
Nice has on average 300 sunny days a year, many important historical sights and museums, a fabulous **Old Town**, and great dining.

The Eastern French Riviera: From Nice to the Italian Border
The French lifestyle with an Italian feel greets you in this part of the French Riviera. Some of the highlights here include the lovely hillop **Eze**, upscale **St-Jean-Cap-Ferrat**, and the quaint harbor town of **Ville-franche-sur-Mer** (*see cover photo*). We'll also visit swanky **Monaco**.

The Western French Riviera: From St-Tropez to Nice
Hilltop villages, art museums, coastal resorts and a **St-Tropez** tan all await you in the western French Riviera. You'll also visit picturesque villages and great beaches in places like **Grimaud**, **Antibes**, and **Cannes**.

The Main Cities of Provence
Arles is one of the three "A's" that make up the most visited cities in Provence (along with Aix-en-Provence and Avignon). Arles has everything you could want in a Provence city: festivals, an Old Town, Roman ruins, cafés and intimate restaurants.

Aix-en-Provence is a graceful and sophisticated city. Between the 12th and 15th centuries it was the capital of Provence. Shaded squares with bubbling fountains in the Old Quarter, 17th-century town houses and the cours Mirabeau (the grand main avenue) make Aix a must for all visitors to Provence.

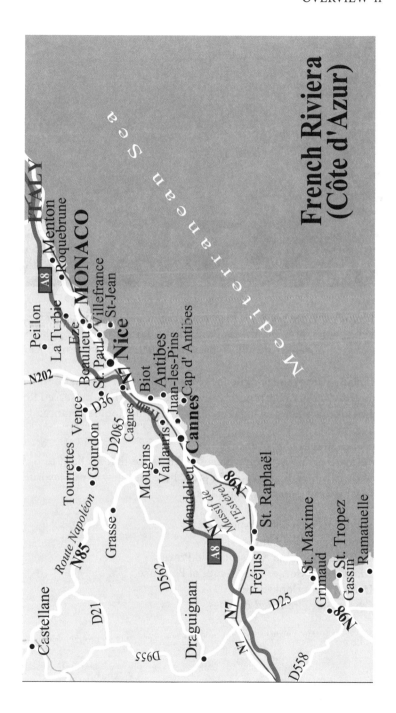

French Riviera
(Côte d'Azur)

Although the last pope left in 1377, you're reminded of the papal legacy everywhere in modern-day **Avignon**. Its large student population makes it a vibrant city unlike most of the small villages of Provence.

Officially part of the Languedoc region, **Nîmes** is a popular destination for visitors to Provence. Some of the world's best-preserved Roman sights are here, giving it the nickname "the Rome of France."

Lovely Villages of Provence

There are so many lovely villages in Provence that it's hard to pick favorites. Depending on your interest, here are a few of our favorites and why we find them so appealing:

- **Saignon:** Quiet and Unspoiled
- **Lourmarin:** Fine Dining
- **Oppède-de-Vieux:** A Taste of Old Provence
- **L'Isle-sur-la-Sorge:** The "Venice of Provence"
- **Uzès:** An Overlooked Gem
- **Cassis:** Sun-Drenched Beaches

Marseille & the Coast
Cosmopolitan and diverse **Marseille,** the breathtaking **Grand Canyon du Verdun,** vineyards and seafront resorts offer the traveler a little bit of everything in this area of Provence.

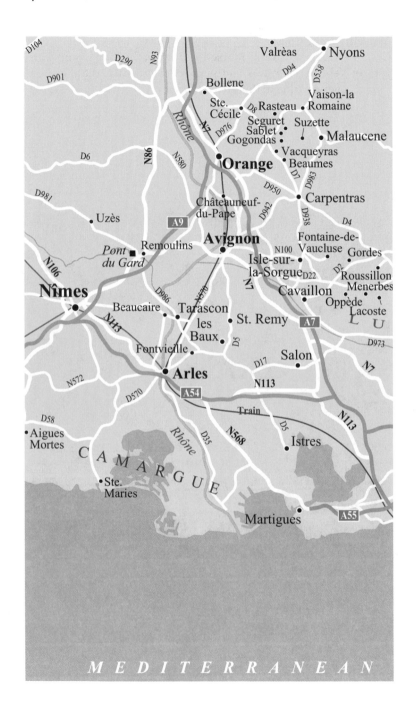

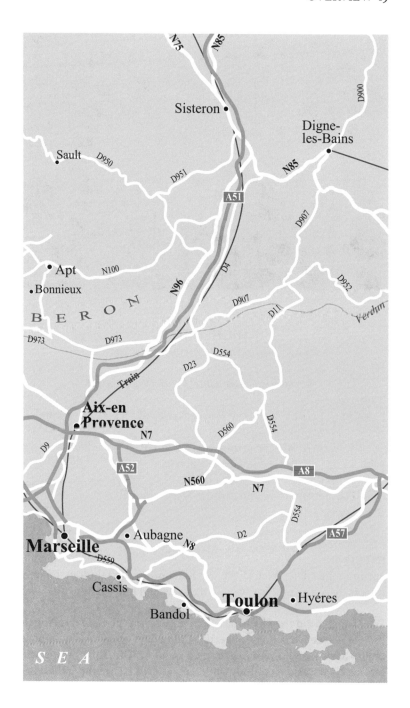

3. Nice

HIGHLIGHTS

• Strolling on the Promenade des Anglais

• Wandering Nice's Old Town (Vieux Nice)

• Chagall paintings at the Musée National Message Biblique

• Avant-garde art at the Musée d'Art Moderne et d'Art Contemporain

• People-watching and dining on the colorful cours Saleya

INTRO

For most travelers, **Nice** is the introduction to the fabulous French Riviera. Nice's airport is the second busiest in France (after Paris).

Why some avoid the city is perplexing. Nice, on the **Baie des Anges** (Bay of Angels), has on average 300 sunny days a year, many important historical sights and museums, a fabulous Old Town, and great dining. Nice was part of Italy until 1860 and you'll see the Italian influence in everything from architecture to cuisine. Yes, it's a large city, but if you simply take time to experience it, you'll learn to love Nice.

COORDINATES

Nice (population 350,000) is in the south of France on the Mediterranean Sea, just 25 miles (40km) from the Italian border. It's 20 miles (33km) northeast of Cannes and 567 miles (912km) south of Paris.

The **Nice-Côte d'Azur Airport** is located on a peninsula 20 minutes west of the central city of Nice. A taxi into town costs at least €40. Buses run every 30 minutes to the central city for €6. Purchase the Aéro Ticket for buses 98 and 99. Bus 99 runs from the airport to the Nice's main train station in 30 minutes. Bus 98 runs along the promenade des Anglais around the Old Town. The buses operate between 6am and 11pm. Check with the helpful staff at the airport bus station in Terminal 1. Once in Nice, hop on a bus or tram to get around town (€1.50 single ride, 10 tickets for €10).

There are also airport express shuttles to Monaco (#110), Cannes (#210), and Antibes (#250). Each runs hourly from Terminal 1. Check out www.lignesdazur.com.

SIGHTS
Promenade des Anglais

This wide boulevard runs four miles along the entire length of **Nice's waterfront.** The name means "walkway of the English" because it was financed by wealthy English tourists who came here in droves in the 1800s in search of sun and sea. Today it's a beautiful walk made all the more interesting by sunbathers, walkers, runners and skaters from so many different parts of the world. Oh, and put your eyes back into your head. While nudity is prohibited, topless bathing is

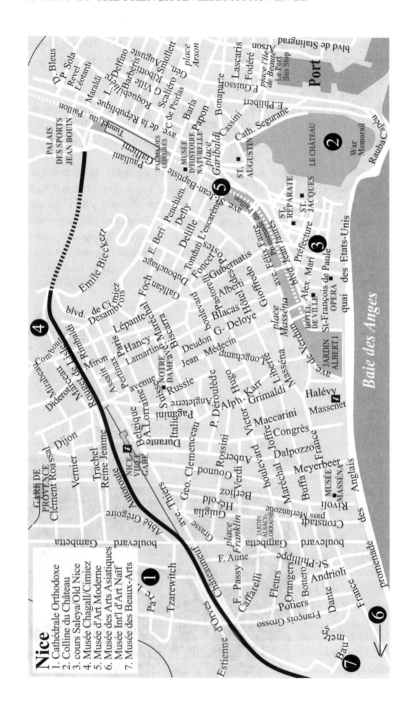

Nice
1. Cathédrale Orthodoxe
2. Colline du Château
3. cours Saleya/Old Nice
4. Musée Chagall/Cimiez
5. Musée d'Art Moderne
6. Musée des Arts Asiatiques
7. Musée Intl d'Art Naïf
7. Musée des Beaux-Arts

not. The beaches here are made up of large uncomfortable rocks. At the east end of the promenade it becomes the **quai des Etats-Unis**. You can head to any number of beach clubs along the promenade. For around €20, you'll get a chair and cushion and waiter service while you relax in the sun. We like **Hi-Beach** and **Castel Plage**. Be warned that waiter service here can be (shall we say) leisurely!

Jardin Albert-1er
The Albert I Garden is a public park that links the Promenade des Anglais with Vieux Nice (Old Town). Developed in the 1800s, you'll find locals and tourists relaxing surrounded by exotic palms and flowers. *Info: avenue de Verdun/avenue des Phocéens. Open daily. Free.*

Cours Saleya
This has been the main street of **Vieux Nice** (Old Town) since the Middle Ages. You must come here if you visit Nice. At times it seems that everyone in Nice is here, especially at night when its restaurants and cafés fill with locals and tourists. It's the home to a wonderful daily flower and food market. On Mondays, it's an antique market. Walk through the maze of narrow streets in Old  Nice past small churches and under drying laundry for photo opportunities at every turn.

Hôtel Negresco
Prominently located on the promenade des Anglais, this hotel is a Nice landmark. Even if you don't dine or drink here, step inside and admire this incredible building. From the lobby, you can visit the Salon Royal with its immense 19th-century Baccarat crystal chandelier and dome. *Info: 37 promenade des Anglais.*

Place Masséna

This beautiful square is named after Jean-André Masséna, one of France's great military heroes. You might feel like you're in Italy rather than France with its rococo buildings. The *place* is elegant with black-and-white pavement and bubbling fountains. The modern art addition features lit men on pedestals high above you. You'll find shopping for all budgets around the square.

Promenade du Paillon

This green parkway connects the Jardin Albert-1er with the **MAMAC** (modern art museum). Filled with palm trees and exotic Mediterranean plants, this is a wonderful addition to Nice's central city.

Musée Masséna

This Belle Époque beachfront villa is filled with painting from French, Italian, and Dutch masters. We especially liked the exhibit of images of Nice throughout the years. Don't miss the lovely garden. *Info: 35 promenade des Anglais/65 rue de France. www.massena-nice.org. Tel. 04/93.91.19.10. Open Wed-Mon 10am-6pm. Closed Tue. Admission: €6.*

Place Rossetti/Cathédrale Ste-Réparate

This elegant square is another example of Nice's connection to Italy. Look around and you might feel as if you're in Milan or Rome instead of in France. On the square is Nice's cathedral. It's another wonderful example of Baroque architecture with intricate plasterwork and elaborate frescoes. The cathedral is named after the patron saint of Nice. She was a teenage virgin whose martyred body is said to have floated to Nice in the 4th century accompanied by angels (really?). This is how the city's Baie des Anges (Bay of Angels) got its name. *Info: place Rossetti. Cathedral closed noon-2pm and most Mon. Admission: Free.*

Musée des Beaux-Arts Jules-Chéret

The Jules-Chéret Fine Arts Museum is housed in a 19th-century mansion. This museum on the west side of

MUSEUM PASS

Nice's municipal museums, which used to be free, now charge admission. You can purchase a €20 seven-day pass for entry to the Modern and Contemporary Art Museum, Fine Arts Museum, Archaeological Museum, and Masséna Museum.

town, contains works of former residents of the city (including those of the man from whom the museum takes its name). Artists on display include Monet, Degas, Sisley, Dufy, Bonnard, and Renoir. There are also ceramic works by Picasso, and sculpture by Rodin. *Info: 33 avenue des Baumettes. Tel. 04/92.15.28.28. Open Tue-Sun 10am-6pm. Closed Mon. Admission: €5.*

Musée d'Art Moderne et d'Art Contemporain (MAMAC)

You can't miss the contemporary structures (four gray marble towers) that house this museum of avant-garde art from the 1960s to today. Works featured here include those by Lichtenstein and Warhol. Check out the fantastic rooftop terrace. *Info: promenade des Arts. www. mamac-nice.org. Tel. 04/97.13.42.01. Open Tue-Sun 10am-6pm. Closed Mon. Admission: €10.*

Colline du Château

High on a rock above the city are the ruins of a castle that was destroyed in 1706. The ruins are now a park and gardens. You have fantastic views of the foothills of the Alps, the bay, the waterfront promenade and the red-tile roofs of Old Nice. You can take an elevator to the top of this hill for free. The elevator is on the quai des Etats-Unis just to the left of the Hôtel Suisse. Elevator operates daily from 10am-7pm (until 8pm in summer). *Info: Colline du Château. Open daily. Admission: Free.*

Cathédrale Orthodoxe Russe St-Nicolas

You'll know when you're getting close to the Russian Orthodox Cathedral as you can't help but notice its onion-shaped domes, so out of place on the Riviera. In 1912, Czar Nicholas II gave the cathedral to the large Russian community who lived and vacationed here. You'll feel like you're in Russia (or at least not in Nice) when you step into its interior, filled with icons and incense. *Info: avenue Nicolas-II at 17 boulevard du Tzaréwitch. Tel. 04/93.96.88.02. Open daily (closed to tourists Sun mornings). Admission: €3. Currently closed for renovations through 2016.*

Musée des Arts Asiatiques

You'll find Asian paintings, sculpture, carvings and ceramics at this museum. It's housed in a sleek modern building built on an artificial lake in the 17-acre Parc Phoenix, a botanical garden. *Info: 405 promenade des Anglais. www.arts-asiatiques.com. Tel. 04/92.29.37.00. Open May to mid-Oct Wed-Mon 10am-6pm (mid-Oct to Apr until 5pm). Closed Tue. Admission: Free.*

Musée International d'Art Naïf Anatole-Jakovsky

This museum is named after an art critic, and houses his collection of over 600 works of naïve art. You'll find everything from primitive paintings to American folk art here. *Info: avenue de Fabron (in the Château St-Héléne). Tel. 04/93.71.78.33. Open Wed-Mon 10am-6pm. Closed Tue. Admission: €6.*

Cimiez

This hilltop neighborhood is located in the northeast part of town. The easiest way to get here (it's about three miles north of Old Nice) is to take bus numbers 15, 17, or 22 from place Masséna. Just off of the square, look for the Masséna Guitry stop on rue Sacha Guitry. It's at the east end of Galeries Lafayette department store. Get off the bus at the Arènes-Matisse stop. You'll find the **Parc des Antiquités** at the top of the hill. This former arena and its gardens contain Roman ruins dating back to the first century.

Cimiez is home to two museums by famous artists with connections to this city.

Musée National Message Biblique–Marc Chagall

Russian painter Marc Chagall (who later became a French citizen) donated the collection at this museum to France, and it's among the largest anywhere. He was often influenced by religious themes, and you'll find his "Biblical Message" on display here. These 12 large paintings illustrate the first two books of the Old Testament. The museum has lovely gardens filled with herbs, olive trees and pools. *Info: avenue du Dr-Ménard (in Cimiez). www.musee-chagall.fr. Tel. 04/93.53.87.20. Open Wed-Mon May-Oct 10am-6pm (Nov-Apr until 5pm. Closed Tue. Admission: €8. Buses #15 and #22 stop at the museum.*

Musée Matisse
The Matisse Museum, located in a 17th-century villa, contains the largest collection of paintings by Henri Matisse, who spent the last years of his life in Nice, and some of his personal effects are on display. Matisse is one of the 20th century's greatest painters. Most of his works here were created while he resided in Nice. Everything from his works as a student to his late-life works – from nudes to religious art – is featured here. Among the famous works are his *Blue Nude IV* and *Nude in Armchair with a Green Plant*. *Info: 164 avenue des Arenes-de-Cimiez (in Cimiez). www.musee-matisee-nice.org. Tel. 04/93.81.08.08. Open Wed-Mon 10am-6pm. Closed Tue. Admission: €10. Buses #15, 17, and 22 stop at the museum.*

Musée Franciscain/Église et Monastère de Cimiez
This sight in Cimiez also has a Matisse connection. This Franciscan monastery is still home to monks. There are lovely gardens with panoramic views (Matisse is buried in the cemetery), a museum dedicated to the history of the Franciscan order, and a 15th-century church with elegant works by Bréa. *Info: place du Monastère (in Cimiez). Tel. 04/93.81.00.04. Museum open Mon-Sat 10am-noon and 3pm-5:30pm. Closed Sun. Admission: Free.*

Musée Archéologique
This archeology museum is filled with Roman finds from the Cimiez area. *Info: 160 avenue des Arènes-de-Cimiez (in Cimiez). Tel. 04/93.81.59.57. Open Wed-Mon 10am-6pm. Closed Tue. Admission: €4.*

The Beaches East of the Port and the Sentier de Mer
One of our favorite places in Nice is an area often ignored by travelers. Past the port (to the east) you'll find boulevard Franck Pilatte. Follow this boulevard along the sea. Look for the signs "Sentier de Mer."

This is a walkway that runs along the sea. There are several small and rocky beaches in this area and restaurants and bars with great views of the city. The path ends at Coco Beach.

A WALK IN NICE'S OLD TOWN

Begin your walk at the **Jardin Albert-1er** on the **promenade des Anglais** between avenue de Verdun and boulevard Jean-Jaurès.

Take in the sunbathers, runners and other walkers on the promenade des Anglais, the waterfront boulevard. Along the promenade is the **Jardin Albert 1er** (Albert I Garden). It's filled with exotic palms and flowers. Here, the promenade becomes the **quai des Etats-Unis**.

As you're heading toward the giant rock, turn left onto **avenue des Phocéens** and take the first right onto **rue St-François-de-Paule.**

You're now in Nice's **Old Town** (Vieux Nice). At number 14 (on your right) is **Alziari**, the place for fragrant olive oil (for sale in many sizes of blue and yellow tins), olive soap and olive spread. On your left at number 9 is the beautiful **Eglise St-François-de-Paule** (also called Eglise des Dominicains), the sight of frequent classical concerts.

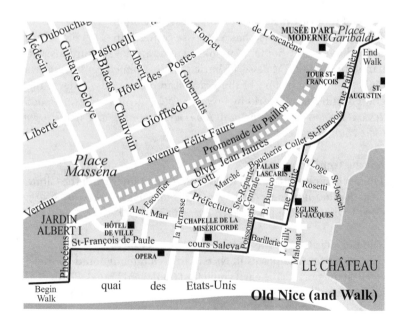

Old Nice (and Walk)

Step inside and admire its beautiful interior. At number 7 (on your left) is the picturesque storefront of **Confiserie Auer** *(see photo on right)*. This candy shop has been in business since 1820 and counts Queen Victoria as one of its famous customers.

At number 4 (on the right) is the opulent **Opéra de Nice**. The four statues on top represent singing, music, dance and theatre, and the opera house is home to Nice's chorus, orchestra, opera and ballet. Charles Garnier, the designer of this building, also created the famous opera house in Paris and the casino in Monte Carlo.

Notice the bilingual street signs are in French and the old Niçois language (an Italian dialect).

Continue down rue St-François-de-Paule to the cours Saleya.

To your left is the **Palais des Ducs de Savoie** (Dukes of Savoy Palace), parts of which date back to 1559. Formerly the home of the kings of Sardinia, Nice's Italian rulers until 1860, it's now police headquarters.

The colorful **cours Saleya** is the main street of Old Nice and has been since the Middle Ages. It's home to a wonderful daily flower and food market. On Mondays, it's an antiques market. Relax at one of the many cafés that line the street.

On your left on the cours Saleya is the **Chapelle de la Miséricorde**. Stop in and take in the chapel's splendor. Filled with chandeliers, faux marble, frescoes, and carved wood, it's one of the world's best examples of the Baroque style. *Info: cours Saleya. Open daily. Admission: Free.*

See that yellow stone building at the end of cours Saleya? Artist **Henri Matisse** lived there from 1921 to 1938.

Before leaving the cours Saleya, sample *socca*, a crêpe made with chickpea flour. There are several places that serve *socca*. One stand is often set up in front of **La Cambuse** restaurant (on the left side of the cours Saleya). Many of the restaurants here also serve the specialty *pissaladière*, a pizza-like tart with onions, black olives and purée of anchovies and sardines

Turn left at **rue de la Poissonnière.**

On this small street is **Eglise Notre-Dame de l'Annonciation** (on your left). Check out the church's elaborate interior. This Baroque church is dedicated to St. Rita, the patron of desperate causes (does she know some of our friends?). Notice the interesting chapel on the right featuring St. Erasmus, the protector of mariners. *Info: 1 rue de la Poissonerie. Open daily. Admission: Free.*

Turn right onto rue de la Préfecture and then left onto rue Droite.

At the intersection of rue Droite and place du Jésus is **Eglise du Jésus** (Gesu). Stop in if you haven't had enough churches. The plain exterior doesn't prepare you for the incredible over-the-top Baroque interior. Notice the wooden pulpit and the carved crucifix extending from it. *Info: Open daily. Admission: Free.*

At 15 rue Droite (on your left) is the sumptuous **Palais Lascaris**, built in the 17th century. There are 15 palaces in Old Town and this is the

best and only one open to the public. The palace is filled with tapestries and statues, and has one of the grandest staircases you'll ever see. *Info: 15 rue Droite. Tel. 04/93.62.72.40. Closed Tue. Admission: €6.*

Continue on rue Droite until it ends and turn right onto rue St-François which turns into rue Pairolière.

You'll pass the **Tour St-François** (Tower of St. Francis) on your left at the square Jardin Auguste Icarte.

Continue down rue Pairolière.

The large square that you enter is **Place Garibaldi** (at rue Cassini). This very Italian-looking square was created at the end of the 18th century. In the center stands a statue and fountain of Joseph Garibaldi, an Italian patriot. You can end your walk here at one of the cafés.

TRAIN TOURISTIQUE

If you don't want to walk to the sights of Nice, try the rubber-wheeled **tourist train** (Train Touristique de Nice). It departs at least once every hour from the Jardin Albert-1er (Albert I Garden) near the waterfront. The trip takes 45 minutes and passes many of Nice's main sights and costs €8 (€4 under age 9). Who cares if you look like a dork? *Info: Tel. 06/08.55.03.30. www.trainstouristiquesdenice.com. Operates daily 10am to 5pm (until 6pm in Apr, May and Sep and until 7pm Jun-Aug).*

BEST SLEEPS & EATS

Hyatt Regency Palais de la Méditerranée €€€
This Art Deco building was renovated in 2004. Fantastic views of the sea from its prime location on the Promenade des Anglais (Nice's seafront street and walkway), near Old Nice. Great outdoor pool. Its restaurant, **Le 3e**, serves Mediterranean cuisine on the poolside terrace. *Info: 13 Promenade des Anglais. www.lepalaisdelamediterranee.com. Tel. 04/93.27.12.34 (hotel)/04/92.14.77.19 (restaurant). V, MC, AE. Restaurant, bar, outdoor pool, AC, TV, telephone, minibar, in-room safe, hairdryer, WiFi.*

La Perouse €€€
This charming hotel is tucked into the hillside below the *château*, just a short walk from Old Nice. Great location, helpful staff, and a lovely pool. *Info: 11 quai Rauba-Capeau. www.hotel-la-perouse.com. Tel. 04/93.62.34.63. V, MC,*

DC, AE. Restaurant, bar, outdoor pool, TV, telephone, minibar, hairdryer, safe, WiFi.

Hôtel Negresco €€€ The grand dame of Nice hotels. Located on the promenade des Anglais, this luxurious hotel will pamper you in style. It's home to the Salon Royal with its immense 19th-century Baccarat crystal chandelier and dome. **Le Chantecler**, Nice's most prestigious restaurant, is also located here. *Info: 37 promenade des Anglais. www.hotel-negresco-nice.com. Tel. 04/93.16.64.00. V, MC, DC, AE. Restaurants, bar, gym, AC, TV, telephone, minibar, hairdryer, WiFi.*

Hôtel Gounod €€
Built in the early 1900s, this 45-room hotel is a good, moderately priced choice in Nice's central city. It's about a five-minute walk to the beach. Comfortable and quiet guest rooms, and an added bonus is that guests can use the pool at the Hôtel Splendid next door. *Info: 3 rue Gounod. www.gounod-nice.fr. Tel. 04/93.16.42.00. V, MC, DC, AE. Restaurant, bar, gym, AC, TV, telephone, minibar, hairdryer, WiFi.*

Hôtel de la Fontaine €€
Located just off the promenade des Anglais and the beach, this 29-room hotel is located on one of Nice's main shopping streets. The hotel was recently refurbished and features anti-allergy flooring, blankets, and pillows. Friendly staff. *Info: 49 rue de France. www.hotel-fontaine.com. Tel. 04/93.88.30.38. V, MC, AE. AC, TV, telephone, hairdryer, safe, WiFi.*

Villa de la Tour €-€€
This small hotel has an excellent location in the Old Town off of the Promenade du Paillon. Rooms are simple and some can be quite small. Although the area is busy with tourists, new windows reduce

the noise level. Staff is very friendly and helpful. The restaurant here, **Le VLT**, is quite good as is the wine bar, **Cave de la Tour**, located across the street. Some rooms have tiny balconies. Public parking is available, but down the street (€24 per day). *Info: 4 rue de la Tour. www. villa-la-tour.com. Tel. 04/93.80.08.15. AC, TV, hairdryer, safe, WiFi.*

Villa Saint-Exupéry €

Budget travelers can stay at this student residence and former monastery in the summer, when it opens its doors to visitors. Both basic rooms and dormitory communal rooms are available. It's located two miles north of the city center. The former chapel is now a popular bar. *Info: 22 ave. Gravier. www.villahostels.com. Tel. 04/93.84.42.83. V, MC. WiFi. There is also another location near the beach at 6 rue Sacha Guitry. Tel. 04/93.16.13.45.*

Riviera Pebbles (Apartments) €-€€€

One great way to truly experience life in the French Riviera is to rent an apartment. They're usually less expensive and larger than a hotel room. If we didn't have to check out hotels, we would always stay in an apartment. Many come with a washer/dryer combination that allows you to pack less. There are many apartments for rent through agencies such as Riviera Pebbles. *Info: www.rivierapebbles.com.*

Le Grand Balcon €€€

You'll find innovative cuisine in a romantic setting at this restaurant. Try the duck in pear sauce or the chicken with chanterelle mush-

rooms in a cream sauce. *Info: 10 rue St-François-de-Paule. www.legrandbalcon. net. Tel. 04/93.62.60.74. Open daily lunch and dinner.*

Le Chantecler €€€

Nice's most prestigious restaurant located in the luxurious Hôtel Negresco. It features such innovative dishes as crab-and-mango cannelloni. *Info: 37 promenade des Anglais. Tel. 04/93.16.64.00. Closed Mon, Tue and Jan to mid-Feb. Reservations required.*

La Merenda €€-€€€

This tiny bistro, run by the former chef at the Hôtel Negresco, has no phone. You have to stop by to make reservations in person, but it's worth it. Innovative cuisine, fresh ingredients and attentive service. *Info: 4 rue Raoul Bosio (formeryl rue de la Terrasse). No phone. No credit cards. Closed weekends, part of Aug, and two weeks at Christmas and New Year's.*

Le Tire Bouchon €€-€€€

This tiny bistro in the Old Town serves the specialties of the South of France. The *cassoulet* (a meat, bean and sausage casserole) is fantastic as is *la souris d'agneau braisée* (lamb shank served in a thyme sauce). Comfortable outdoor seating on the pedestrian street is also available. *Info: 19 rue de la Préfecture. www.le-tire-bouchon.com. Tel. 04/93.92.63.64. Open daily for dinner. Lunch daily Sep-May.*

La Part des Anges €-€€

Organic and biodynamic wines are gaining in popularity worldwide, and especially in France. This small wine shop and wine bar has a good selection of organic wines that you can down with *charcuterie* or cheese plates. There's also a small selection of hot dishes (the house specialty is pasta with razor clams). There's also a second location, La Mise en Verre, at 17 rue Pastorelli. *Info: 17 rue Gubernatis (in the New Town off of rue Pastorelli). www.la-part-des-anges-nice.fr. Tel 04/93.62.69.80. Closed Sun. Tel. 04/93.85.69.90. Closed Sat (lunch) and Sun (lunch).*

Le Safari €€

Dine on Provençal and Niçoise specialties at this popular restaurant overlooking the flower market. We have eaten here frequently and never had a bad meal. The people-watching is great. The gnocchi du jour is always a good choice as is the *daube à la niçoise* (beef stew with

red wine, tomatoes, and onions). This is the best of the touristy restaurants along the cours Saleya. *Info: 1 cours Saleya. www.restaurantsafari.fr. Tel. 04/93.80.18.44. Open daily.*

Pasta Basta €
Good, hearty pasta dishes and pizza (and not a bad house wine either). *Info: 18 rue de la Préfecture. Tel. 04/93.80.03.57. Open daily.*

Il Vicoletto €€
This Italian restaurant is one block inland from the promenade des Anglais and near the Musée Masséna. You can dine outside along the pedestrian street or in the cozy restaurant. Try the *ravioli farciti verdure al burro e salvia* (ravioli stuffed with vegetables in a butter and sage sauce) or the garlicky *linguine alle vongole* (linguine with clams in a white wine sauce). The real deal here is the decent Italian house wine at €10. *Info: 6 bis. Rue de France. Tel. 04/93.87.30.55. Open daily.*

La Rossettisserie €-€€
A rotisserie grill where you can watch your beef, chicken, pork, duck, veal, or lamb being cooked on the spit. Each meal is served with a choice of baked potatoes, mashed potatoes, or vegetable *ratatouille*. Located in Old Town near place Rossetti. Noisy and fun. *Info: 8 rue Mascoïnat. www.larossettisserie.com. Tel. 04/93.76.18.80. Open daily for lunch and dinner.*

L'Atelier du Port €€
We absolutely love this modern and sleek restaurant in the area north of the port. The eateries in this neighborhood are filled with mostly locals and this area is a good alternative to the touristy restaurants in Old Town. Friendly waiters deliver large chalkboard menus in English or French. You can watch your food being prepared in the open kitchen. Excellent Provençal wine list and delicious dishes such as *cocotte de veau* (veal casserole) or the *ravioli citron* (ravioli sweetened with lemons from Menton on the Italian border). Save room for the excellent desserts like *tarte tatin* and *mousse. Info: 45 rue Bonaparte (at rue Bavastro). Tel. 09/83.03.88.44. Open daily. No lunch Sun.*

La Réserve €€€
If you're going to splurge for dinner in Nice, this is our choice. This restaurant is located east of the Port de Nice. It offers stunning panoramic views of the Bay of Angels (*see photo on next page*) from its unique location with terraces overlooking the sea. Young chef Sébastien Mahuer serves sophisticated and innovative cuisine. You'll love dining at this Art Deco restaurant. Truly an experience. Opt for the

Menu Riviera at €55. *Info: 60 blvd Franck Pilatte. www.lareservedenice. fr. Tel. 04/97.08.14.80. Open daily for lunch and dinner. No dinner Sun.*

Glacier Fenocchio
Try some of the best ice cream in the world. This family-owned institution has two locations in Old Nice. The main shop is at 2 place Rossetti facing the Cathédrale de Ste-Réparate. A second shop is just off the cours Saleya at 6 rue de la Poissonerie. Be adventurous and try one of the unique flavors like lavender, tomato, jasmin, or *comté de nice* (studded with pine nuts and candied mandarin). *Info: Tel. 04/93.80.72.52 (place Rossetti)/04/93.62.88.80 (rue de la Poissonerie). Open 9am to midnight. Poissonerie location closed Tue.*

BEST SHOPPING
La Promenade des 100 Antiquaires
There are many antique shops on **rue Catherine Ségurane** and **rue Emmanuel Philibert.** Les Puces de Nice has 30 stalls under one roof on Quai Lunel (on Port de Nice). On each third Saturday of the month, there's an antique market on place Garibaldi. *Info: www.niceantic.com. Closed Sun.*

Galeries Lafayette
This upscale department store has a wonderful food court in the basement and a restaurant on the fourth floor. *Info: 6 avenue Jean Médelin (near place Masséna). Tel. 04/92.17.36.36. Open daily.*

Confiserie Henri-Auer
This fantastic candy and chocolate shop near the opera house has been in business since 1820. *Info: 7 rue St-François-de-Paule. Tel. 04/93.62.94.03. Closed Sun and Mon.*

cours Saleya
The colorful cours Saleya (the main street of Old Nice) has a wonderful **daily flower and food market.** On Mondays, it's an antiques market.

If you want to shop, try one of these boutique-lined streets: rue Paradis, rue de Verdun, rue Masséna, and avenue Jean-Médecin.

BEST NIGHTLIFE & ENTERTAINMENT

Le Relais
If you're looking for an elegant place to have a cocktail, try the bar at the Hôtel Negresco. *Info: 37 promenade des Anglais. Tel. 04/93.16.64.00.*

Wayne's
Noisy bar with occasional live performances. It's popular with English-speaking tourists and students. *Info: 15 rue de la Prefecture. Tel. 04/93.13.46.99.*

Casino Palais de Mediterranée
You can gamble the night away at this elegant casino located on the waterfront. Slot machines from 10am. Gaming tables from 8pm. *Info: 15 promenade des Anglais. www.casinomediterranee.com. Tel. 04/92.14.68.00. Open daily from 10am-3am.*

Le Ruhl Casino
Recently renovated, you can also gamble the night away at this flashy casino located on the waterfront. There are more than 300 slot machines. *Info: 1 promenade des Anglais. www.lucienbarriere.com. Tel. 04/97.03.12.22. Open daily from 9am-4am (until 5am in summer).*

Les Trois Diables
On the cours Saleya, the main street of Old Nice. A bar and dance club. Popular happy hour. *Info: 2 cours Saleya. www.lesdiables.com. Tel. 06/62.27.47.17. Open daily.*

Opéra de Nice
This opulent opera house was designed by Charles Garnier, who also designed the famous opera house in Paris and the casino in Monte Carlo. The four statues on top represent singing, music, dance and theatre, and the opera house is home to

> **EVENTS IN NICE**
> Two events are very big in Nice: **Carnaval**, Nice's Mardi Gras, takes place the weeks leading up to Ash Wednesday; and the **Nice Jazz Festival**, which is held for a week in mid-July. *Info: www.nice-jazzfestival.fr*

Nice's chorus, orchestra, opera and ballet *(see photo below)*. *Info: 4 rue St-François-de-Paule. Tel. 04/92.17.40.00. Open for performances. www. opera-nice.org.*

High Club
You'll pay €20 to enter this dance club with three floors. *Info: 45 promenade des Anglais. www.highclub.fr. Tel. 06/16.95.75.87. open Fri-Sun 11:45pm-6am.*

Le GLAM
Nice's favorite gay nightclub features techno and dance music. There are regular themed parties, including drag shows. *Info: 6 rue Eugène Emmanuel. Tel. 06/60.55.26.61. Thu-Sun 11pm-5am.*

Nice is an extremely popular destination for the LGBT community. There are a number of popular **gay establishments** in Nice. Here are just a few:

- **Red Kafe**, *9 rue Halévy, Tel. 04/89.97.47.93 (bar)*
- **Le 6**, *6 rue Raoul Bosio, Tel. 04/93.62.66.54 (bar)*
- **Le Bar Bitch**, *2 rue Rossetti, Tel. 06/18.01.72.63 (bar/café)*
- **Le Gossip**, *7 rue Bonnaparte, Tel. 04/83.45.72.15 (bar)*
- **Les Bains Douches**, *7 rue Gubernalis, Tel. 04/93.80.28.26 (sauna)*
- **Le Malabar**, *10 rue Bonaparte, Tel. 09/51.18.53.52 (bar and café)*
- **Le Morgan**, *3 rue Claudia, Tel. 04/93.86.86.08 (cruising bar)*
- **Le Code**, *4 rue Papon, Tel. 09/81.76.86.00 (cruising bar).*

4. The Eastern French Riviera

HIGHLIGHTS

- Slow down in St-Jean-Cap-Ferrat

- An ideal town on the sea: Villefranche-sur-Mer

- Magnificent Eze, peaceful La Turbie, and sedate Menton

- Glitzy Monaco

INTRO

The French lifestyle with an Italian feel greets you in this part of the French Riviera. The eastern half of the **Côte d'Azur** offers great beaches, beautiful hilltop villages and renowned gardens.

We'll visit villages east of Nice up to the border and reaching down to the sea. Some of the highlights here include the lovely hilltop village **Eze**, upscale **St-Jean-Cap-Ferrat**, and the quaint harbor town of

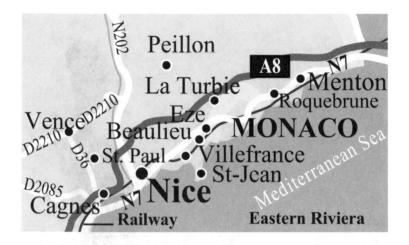

Villefranche-sur-Mer. Visit the unique principality of **Monaco,** or shoot over the border and visit **Ventimiglia** in Italy to eat lunch or shop!

COORDINATES

The **Eastern French Riviera** is in the south of France and stretches from the Italian border to Nice along the Mediterranean Sea. The area is about 600 miles (966km) south of Paris. Bus #100 is the best deal if you're using public transportation. It runs from Nice's port (Le Port stop) all the way to Menton on the Italian border. Stops include Villefranche-sur-Mer, Beaulieu-sur-Mer, St-Jean-Cap-Ferrat, Eze-Bord-de-Mer, and Monaco. It doesn't matter how far you travel, the cost is €1.50 each way. Bus #81 also serves Villefranche-sur-Mer, Beaulieu-sur-Mer, and St-Jean-Cap-Ferrat for €1.50 each way.

There's a **coastal rail line** that runs from Ventimiglia on the Italian border (Vintimille in French) to Marseille. There are trains that run nearly every hour on this line. Stops on this scenic train ride include: Menton, Cap-Martin, Monaco, Èze-sur-Mer (not to be confused with hilltop Èze), Beaulieu, St-Jean-Cap-Ferrat, Villefranche-sur-Mer, Nice, Antibes and Cannes. Local trains serve many Provence and Riviera towns. You must validate (*composter*) your ticket at a machine (watch locals do it) before you get on a SNCF train.

VILLEFRANCHE-SUR-MER

Villefranche-sur-Mer is a wonderful harbor town, 6 miles (10 km) east of Nice. Bus #100 departs from the port in Nice (Le Port stop) about every 15 minutes. Get off at the Octroi stop to head down to Villefranche-sur-Mer. The cost of the bus ride (which takes less than a half hour) is only €1.50 each way. Note that the last bus returns to Nice around 8pm. Bus #81 also serves Villefranche-sur-Mer, Beaulieu-sur-Mer, and St-Jean-Cap-Ferrat for €1.50 each way. The train station (with service from most French Riviera towns) is a pleasant 15-minute walk along the water to the Old Town.

The city looks Italian with its yellow and ochre homes reaching down the hill to the sea. The beach here is pebbly, and the deep harbor (located between Nice and Cap Ferrat) can accommodate huge vessels. It's a popular destination for cruise ships.

The interesting rue Obscure, a street that runs parallel to the waterfront, is covered by vaulted arcades (it's just off rue de l'Église). This "Dark Street" served as a bomb shelter during World War II.

The town has a huge restored citadel (**Citadelle St- Elme**) dating from the 16th-century, housing municipal offices and free museums dedicated to local history and art.

There are **markets** in the Old Town at place Amélie Pollonais. Sunday features antiques (search out the old travel posters). On Saturday there is an organic food market. From Monday to Friday you'll find local crafts, arts, and an interesting flea market.

Jean Cocteau decorated the walls of **Chapelle St-Pierre**, a Romanesque church, in the 1950s with surrealist works that include images of St. Peter. *Info: quai de la Douane/place Pollonais/*

rue des Marinières. Tel. 04/93.76.90.70. Closed Tue and mid-Nov to mid-Dec. Admission: €3. There are explanations of the art in English.

Just a few blocks up from the harbor in Old Town is **Eglise St-Michel**. This Baroque church features an 18th-century pipe organ and a stirring statue of Jesus carved from a fig tree. *Info: Place Poullan. Open daily. Admission: Free.*

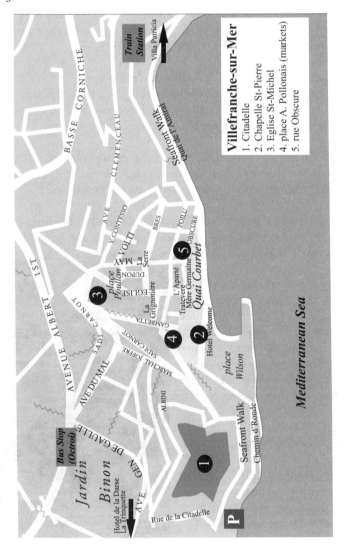

Villefranche-sur-Mer

1. Citadelle
2. Chapelle St-Pierre
3. Eglise St-Michel
4. place A. Pollonais (markets)
5. rue Obscure

HIKING/WALKING

If you like to walk or hike, Villefranche offers many opportunities.

A walkway along the sea connects the Old Town with the Port de la Darse. As you walk down from the bus stop or road, you'll walk along the Citadelle and at the base turn left to take the walkway to the Old Town.

You can also walk along the sea past the train station for great views of the town. If you're really adventurous, take the 50-minute walk to St-Jean-Cap-Ferrat. You'll need to pass the train station on the small beach lane and then climb the stairs at the end of the beach and walk parallel to the tracks on avenue Bordes. Pass the fabulous villas and take a first right. Watch for the signs to the Villa Rothschild.

BEST SLEEPS & EATS

Hôtel Welcome €€-€€€ This former villa has been renovated into a comfortable hotel. All 36 rooms have balconies with views of the port. There is a lively restaurant (€€) and wine bar, and it's an excellent location for exploring the town. *Info: 1 quai Amiral-Courbet. www.welcomehotel.com. Tel. 04/93.76.27.62. V, MC, AE. Restaurant, bar, AC, TV, minibar, hairdryer, safe, WiFi.*

Hôtel de la Darse €
This 21-room hotel is the budget choice in Villefranche. It's located just a little outside of the center of town, so you'll do some walking to get to and from the Old Town. You'll be rewarded for all that walking with excellent sea views. Rooms with garden views are cheapest. *Info: 32 ave. Général de Gaulle. www.hoteldeladarse.com. Tel. 04/93.01.72.54. Bar, AC, TV, hairdryer, WiFi.*

Villa Patricia €-€€

This 10-room seaside hotel is a good choice if you're planning to explore nearby towns by car. Rooms are small (this is France, after all) and clean. There's a lounge where guests can relax. An added bonus is the free parking. It's just a 10-minute walk from Villefranche's Old Town. Owners Franck and Joelle are extremely helpful. The hotel is located below the Basse Corniche road. *Info: 310 ave. de l'Ange Gardien. www.hotel-patricia-riviera.fr. Tel. 04/93.01.06.70. TV, WiFi. No AC.*

La Mère Germaine €€€

Restaurant on the waterfront specializing in grilled fish dishes. This is the choice for formal dining on the harbor. Try the lobster salad. *Info: quai Courbet. www.meregermaine.com. Tel. 04/93.01.71.39. Closed mid-Nov to Dec.*

La Grignotière €€

This friendly restaurant is located near the marketplace and serves local specialties. Delicious pasta dishes, especially spaghetti with shrimp *(gambas)*. *Info: 3 rue du Poilu. Tel. 04/93.76.79.83. Closed Wed. (except in summer). No lunch.*

Le Serre €-€€

You'll find this family-run restaurant located in the Old Town near the Eglise St-Michael. You can choose from an assortment of pizzas or one of the specialties like *daube à la niçoise* (beef stew with red wine, tomatoes, and onions). The three-course menu is a good value at €17. *Info: 16 rue de May. Tel. 04/93.76.79.91. Closed Mon and Tue.*

Trastevere €€

This is our favorite restaurant on the harbor. Whether you're having a simple pizza or a delicious pasta dish, you will not be disappointed. Watch locals and tourists departing from boats on the harbor while you sip a glass of Provençal wine. *Info: 7 quai de l'Amiral Courbet. Tel. 04/93.01.94.26.*

L'Aparté €€- €€€

Located on the interesting medieval rue Obscure, this modern French restaurant serves innovative cuisine. Try the delicious herb-crusted lamb. The wine list features wine from throughout France. *Info: 1 rue Obscure. Tel. 04/93.01.84.88. No lunch. Closed Mon.*

La Trinquette €- €€
Located at the Port de la Darse (on the other side of the Citadelle from Old Town), this café/restaurant serves locals and tourists in an unpretentious setting along the port. An added bonus is frequent live music. *Info: 30 ave. Général de Gaulle. www.restaurant-trinquette-villefranche.com. Tel. 04/93.16.92.48. Closed Wed in winter. Closed Jan.*

ST-JEAN-CAP-FERRAT

We're going to slow down in St-Jean-Cap-Ferrat, 1 mile (2 km) south of Beaulieu/6 miles (10 km) east of Nice.

DRIVING AROUND

The **coastline east of Nice** is a huge cliff with three parallel highways (note: if you want to travel at high speeds from the Italian border all the way past Cannes, making day trips easy, take Route A8):

Grande Corniche – the highest and fastest, with the fewest places to enjoy the view.

Moyenne Corniche – the middle road offering shore views and passing through several towns, including the beautiful and popular Èze.

Basse Corniche – the lowest where you might crawl (especially in July and August) through one picturesque resort after another.

The residents of this port village on the peninsula Cap-Ferrat live here for its warm climate and beautiful sea views. Its promenades are lined with cafés and restaurants, and its port is filled with pleasure craft. It's home to luxurious hotels including the **Grand Hôtel du Cap-Ferrat**, located at the tip of the peninsula. Most of the villas are hidden by gates and lush vegetation. Unlike nearby towns, the pace here is not at all hectic. The beaches here are pebbly, not sandy, and there's a coastal walkway if you want to walk around the cape.

While here, visit the **Villa Ephrussi de Rothschild/Musée Ile-de-France,** a palace by the sea (*photo on next page*). This Italian-style villa was left to the French government by Baroness Rothschild, and includes over 5,000 works of art. Fabulous gardens with ornamental lakes and waterfalls surround the villa. *Info: avenue Denis-Séméria. www.villa-ephrussi.com. Tel. 04/93.01.33.09. Open daily mid-Feb to Oct 10am-6pm (Jul and Aug until 7pm). Nov-mid to Feb Mon-Fri 2pm-6pm,*

Sat and Sun 10am-6pm. Admission: €13. Combined admission with Villa Kérylos (in nearby Beaulieu-sur-Mer) is €20.

BEST SLEEPS & EATS

Grand Hôtel du Cap-Ferrat (Four Seasons) €€€

Luxurious white palace set in the middle of a 17-acre wooded estate and subtropical gardens. Its exclusive location is at the tip of the Cap-Ferrat peninsula. Every amenity you can imagine is here. A nice bonus: great views of the sea from its clifftop pool. *Info: St-Jean-Cap-Ferrat. www.grand-hotel-cap-ferrat.com. Tel. 04/93.76.50.50 (800/525-4800). V, MC, DC, AE. Restaurant, bar, outdoor pool, TV, telephone, minibar, hairdryer, safe, WiFi.*

Hotel Brise Marine €€

Lovely yellow hotel located in a former villa with a fantastic porch and patio overlooking the water. Great place to unwind. Rooms are comfortable and casual. Highly recommended. *Info: 58 avenue Jean Mermoz. www.hotel-brisemarine.com. Tel. 04/93.76.04.36. V, MC, DC, AE. Bar, TV, telephone, WiFi.*

Capitaine Cook €€-€€€
Hearty Provençal dining indoors and outdoors on the patio. This is a family-run restaurant specializing in fish dishes. Try the delicious salmon ravioli. *Info: 11 av. Jean-Mermoz. Tel. 04/93.76.02.66. Closed Wed and Thu lunch. Closed Wed dinner.*

Le Sloop €€-€€€
You can't miss the blue-and-white décor of this portside restaurant. Fish dishes are featured at the indoor and outdoor tables. Excellent *soupe de poisson* (fish soup). *Info: On the port. Tel. 04/93.01.48.63. No lunch Wed in summer. Closed Wed in winter.*

BEAULIEU-SUR-MER

Beaulieu-sur-Mer is just two miles (four km) east of Villefranche-sur-Mer.

This village is referred to as "La Petite Afrique" (Little Africa) owing to its warm climate and lush vegetation. The Alpes-Maritimes mountains descending to the coast shelter this resort town. The stroll along the seafront promenade lets you glimpse lovely villas, most of which are hidden by vegetation and fences. The Art Deco **Casino de Beaulieu** was built in 1903 (no beach attire). The town has two churches, the 12th-century chapel **Santa Maria de Olivo**, and the 19th-century **Eglise du Sacré-Coeur**.

In a town with incredible villas, the **Villa Kérylos** stands out. Step inside for a look. It's an imitation of a Greek villa from Classical times, and contains some Greek antiquities brought here in 1900 when the villa was built by an archeologist. Definitely unusual! *Info: rue Gustave-Eiffel (at the tip of the bay). www.villa-kerylos.com. Tel. 04/93.01.01.44.*

Open daily mid-Feb to Oct 10am-6pm (Jul and Aug until 7pm). Nov to mid-Feb Mon-Fri 2pm-6pm, Sat and Sun 10am-6pm). Admission: €11.50 (with audio guide). Combined admission with Villa Ephrussi (in nearby St-Jean-Cap-Ferrat) is €20.

BEST SLEEPS & EATS

La Pignatelle €€

Dine indoors or outdoors with locals at this restaurant located off of the main street. Nothing fancy here. Featured dishes include *gibelotte de laupin* (rabbit stew) and *tartare de saumon* (salmon tartar). A good deal in expensive Beaulieu. *Info: 10 rue de Quincenet. www.lapignatelle. fr. Tel. 04/93.01.03.37. Closed Wed.*

La Reserve de Beaulieu €€€

The luxury hotel in lovely Beaulieu. This hotel, with a pink-and-white exterior and marble lobby welcomes guests who want to be pampered. It's known for its spa. Every amenity imaginable is available. The highlight is the fabulous 2000-square-foot pool and the sun deck

overlooking the sea. Most rooms have balconies where you can take in the Mediterranean Sea. *Info: 5 Boulevard du Marechal Leclerc. www. reservebeaulieu.fr. Tel. 04/93.01.00.01. V, MC, AE. Spa, restaurants, bar, AC, TV, safe, minibar, WiFi.*

La Reserve also is known for its restaurants and bars. Our favorite is the pool bar with its idyllic setting overlooking the sea and coast. You'll pay for your lunch and drinks here, but it's truly a fantastic setting. Pool bar is open daily 9am-6pm. The formal **Gordon Bennett Bar**, with plush chairs and wood paneling, also serves food and drink. Elegant (and expensive) dining is served at the other restaurants: **Restaurant des Rois** (award-winning restaurant), **La Table de la Réserve** (bistro), and **Vent Debout** (summer restaurant).

Le Havre Bleu €

There are plenty of luxury hotels in Beaulieu, but this is not one of them. Renovated in 2013, this small hotel, with blue shutters, offers simple rooms in a central location. Ask for a room with a terrace or patio. Excellent value. *Info: 29 blvd. Maréchal Joffre. Tel. 04/93.01.01.40. www.lehavrebleu.com. V, MC, AE. Bar, AC, TV, WiFi.*

EZE

Eze is 4 miles (7 km) west of Monte Carlo/7 miles (11 km) east of Nice (via the Moyenne Corniche).

To say that Eze has a magnificent hilltop location is an understatement. This tiny fortified village towers over the surrounding countryside with unbelievable views of the sea. It's the highest of the area's perched villages. You'll enter through the town gate (designed to keep the Turks out). Most of this rocky village dates back to the 14th century. On your way to the top is the tiny **Chapelle de la Ste-Croix**, the former seat of a lay brotherhood that wore white habits and performed good deeds The church of **Notre-Dame de l'Assomption** (built in 1764) has a Baroque interior. A web of narrow streets passes stone houses converted to boutiques, galleries and souvenir shops. It's touristy and, in high season, the narrow streets can get quite cramped, but the view from the hilltop castle ruins are worth it.

For the adventurous, there's a walk on an old mule trail from Eze to **Eze-Bord-de-Mer** on the coast. Look for signs for **Sentier Fédéric Nietzsche.** You begin at the entry to town (just to the left of the entrance to the luxury hotel Château de la Chèvre d'Or). The walk takes at least an hour each way and although beautiful, is only for the fit. If you're not up to the entire walk, just head down a bit for a great view of the coast.

Make sure to visit the **Jardin Exotique** at the hilltop castle ruins (*see photo on page 35*). This densely planted flower and cactus garden (with English descriptions), along with whimsical statuary, affords spectacular views. Don't miss it! *Info: Tel. 04/93.41.10.30. Open daily 9am-sunset. Admission: €6.*

BEST SLEEPS & EATS

Château Eza €€€

This former residence of Prince William of Sweden is now an elegant hotel built into the medieval walls. Donkeys carry your luggage up the narrow and steep cobblestone street. There are only 10 rooms. Extraordinary views. *Info: Rue de la Pise. www.chateaueza.com. Tel. 04/93.41.12.24. V, MC, DC, AE. Restaurant, bar, AC, TV, telephone, minibar, in-room safe, hairdryer, WiFi.*

Hostellerie du Château de la Chèvre d'Or €€€

This incredible luxury-hotel complex of stone houses has 32 rooms. Its secluded setting with narrow alleys has great views of the sea. Truly a unique (and expensive) vacation experience. Its restaurants and

outdoor cliffside bar are just the place to splurge. Fabulous infinity pool. *Info: rue du Barri. www.chevredor.com. Tel. 04/92.10.66.66. V, MC, DC, AE. Restaurant, bar, gym, AC, TV, telephone, minibar, in-room safe, hairdryer.*

La Vieille Maison €€

This family restaurant is located in the seafront town of Eze-sur-Mer. It's a rarity in the area around Eze as it's reasonably priced. Regional dishes are served with affordable local wines. Dine on the rooftop terrace with great views. Known for their *moules* (mussels) and delicious *frites* (French fries served with mayonnaise). *Info: 18 ave. de la Liberté in Èze-Bord-de-Mer. Tel. 04/93.01.58.30. Closed Sun.*

Restaurant de la Chèvre d'Or €€€
This award-winning restaurant in the Hostellerie du Château de la Chèvre d'Or is one of the best in the French Riviera. The menu features innovative Mediterranean dishes prepared by its star chef. The wine cellar boasts over 20,000 bottles from throughout France. Marble floors, cherry wood paneling, impeccable service, and magnificent panoramic views all add to the experience. *Info: Hostellerie du Château de la Chèvre d'Or. www.chevredor.com. Reservations required. Tel. 04/92.10.66.60. Closed Dec to mid-Mar.*

This hotel is also a great place to have a drink at sunset at the **outdoor cliffside hotel bar.** But be warned – there's a steep minimum drink order on weekends. *Info: rue du Barri. Tel. 04/92.10.66.66. Closed mid-Nov to Feb.*

MONACO
Monaco, the capital of glitz, is 12 miles (19 km) east of Nice. Bus#100 connects Monaco to Nice and Menton (and points between) for €1.50. The bus departs from Le Port stop in Nice at the Port de Nice (at the top of the Port across from the church Notre-Dame du Port). The bus runs every 15 minutes. By train, you can reach Monaco from Nice (two per hour/20-minute trip), Villefranche (two per hour/10-minute trip), Antibes (two per hour/50-minute trip), and Cannes (two per hour/70-minute trip).

Monaco mixes aristocratic glitz and a little bit of Las Vegas. It's the second-smallest state in Europe; only Vatican City is smaller. This principality is bordered by France and the Mediterranean Sea, takes up less than one square mile, and is nestled against mountains that seem to push it into the sea. High-rises attest to the fact

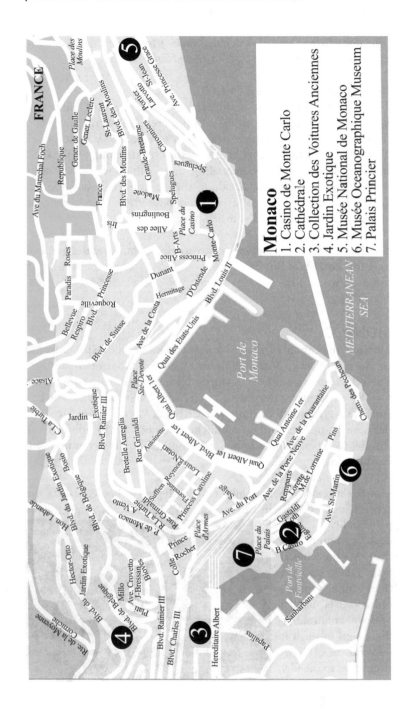

Monaco
1. Casino de Monte Carlo
2. Cathédrale
3. Collection des Voitures Anciennes
4. Jardin Exotique
5. Musée National de Monaco
6. Musée Oceanographique Museum
7. Palais Princier

that there's nowhere to go but up in this tiny country. Residents (Monégasques), of which there are less than 10,000, pay no taxes.

There are four parts of the principality: **Monte Carlo**, home to the famous casino and ultra-luxury hotels; **Fontvieille**, an industrial suburb; **Monaco-Ville**, the location of government buildings and the royal palace; and **La Condamine**, at the port where most Monégasques live. Monaco's location is fantastic, its weather incredible (on average, 310 sunny days a year) and crime is virtually unheard of (there's one policeman for every 100 residents).

Bus service is available within Monaco for €2 (6 tickets for €11, day pass €5.50), with stops at every tourist sight. To figure out which one to take, simply look at the name on the front of the bus.

SIGHTS
Head to the **Place du Palais**. This square offers views of the palace and contains a **statue of Francesco Grimaldi**. Francesco (they refer to him as François here) was an Italian who was kicked out of Genoa.

GRACE KELLY
American film star **Grace Kelly** met Prince Rainier of Monaco while attending the Cannes International Film Festival to promote the Alfred Hitchcock film *To Catch a Thief*, which she starred in with Cary Grant. The film featured her racing along the Corniches. Soon after, in 1956, she married Prince Rainier, moved to Monaco, and had three children with him. Princess Grace was wildly popular among the Monégasques. Ironically, in 1982 she was killed while driving on the same Corniches featured in her film. The flower-decked tomb of Princess Grace is located at **Cathédrale de l'Immaculée-Conception**, a Romanesque-style church, which was also the site of her fairy-tale wedding to Prince Rainier in 1956. Prince Rainier was buried at her side in 2005. *Info: avenue St-Martin. Open daily. Admission: Free.*

He and his cohorts dressed up as monks in 1297 and seized the castle. This was the beginning of the Grimaldi dynasty, which continues to this day.

You can't miss **Le Rocher** (The Rock), crowned by the Prince's Palace. A medieval castle once stood where the **Palais Princier** is located. In the summer you can take a guided tour through the royal family's extravagant home. Included in the tour is a glimpse of the immense art collection, the throne room, the **royal apartments** (*Les Grands Appartements*) and the beautiful state portrait of Princess Grace. You can watch the colorful changing of the guard at around 11:45am to noon. *Info: place du Palais. www.palais.mc. Tel. 377/93.25.18.31. Royal apartments: Open Apr-Oct 10am-6pm (Jul and Aug until 7pm. Closed Nov-Mar. Admission: €8. Combined ticket for Royal Apartments and Oceanography Museum (below) is €19.*

The **Musée Océanographique** (Oceanography Museum), built in 1910, hangs from a cliff in Monaco-Ville. It's sometimes referred to as the Cousteau Aquarium, as Jacques Cousteau, the famous sea-explorer, directed the aquarium until 1988. In addition to its huge (over 90 tanks) and interesting aquarium, the museum contains skeletons of sea creatures (including a giant whale), submarines, and exhibits on the history of sea exploration. *Info: avenue St-Martin. www.oceano. mc. Tel. 377/93.15.36.00. Open daily Jul and Aug 9:30am-8pm, Apr-Jun and Sep 10am-7pm, Oct-Mar 10am-6pm. Admission: €14, €10 under 18, €7 under 13. Combined ticket for Royal Apartments (above) and Oceanography Museum is €19.*

An exotic garden with thousands of cacti and succulents, **Jardin Exotique** features incredible views of the coast are included in the admission price. *Info: boulevard du Jardin Exotique. www.jardin-exotique.mc. Tel. 377/93.15.29.80. Open daily May-Sep 9am-7pm (Feb-Apr and Oct until 6pm, Nov-Jan until 5pm). Admission: €7.20.*

At the **Nouveau Musée National de Monaco**, there are rotating exhibits (with an emphasis on artists who visited Monaco and on the history of Monaco) held at two locations. Villa Sauber is located in a luxurious villa (designed by the same man who designed the Casino de Monte Carlo). *Info: Villa Sauber is east of the casino at 17 avenue Princess Grace. Tel. 377/93.30.91.26. Villa Paloma is next to the Jardin Exotique* *at 56 blvd. du Jardin. Tel. 377/98.98.48.60. Both open daily Jun-Sep 11am-7pm, Oct-May 8am-6pm. Admission: €6. Free first Sun of the month. Combined ticket with Jardin Exotique (above) €10. www.nmnm.mc.*

Visit the **Collection des Voitures Anciennes** to see the royal collection of over 100 automobiles. Now do they need both a Rolls Royce and a Lamborghini? *Info: Les Terrasses de Fontvieille. Tel. 377/92.05.28.56. Open daily 10am-6pm. Admission: €6.50.*

Okay, the **Hôtel de Paris** at the place du Casino is a hotel, not a sight. Or is it? Even if you can't afford to stay here or even eat or drink here, you should at least pop in and be dazzled by the magnificent domed entrance. The palatial lobby is a masterpiece of stained glass, statues, crystal chandeliers and marble pillars. It's said that if you rub the raised knee of the bronze statue of Louis XIV's horse in the lobby, you'll have good luck.

SHOPPING & GAMBLING

There's **great shopping** in Monaco. Main shopping streets include **boulevard des Moulins** (the main street of Monte Carlo), **rue Princess-Caroline** (everything from clothing to baked goods) and **rue Grimaldi** (the main shopping street of the La Condamine area). At **place d'Armes** there is an indoor and outdoor market (every morning).

If you want to shop and feel good about parting with your cash, check out **Boutique du Rocher** with two shops, at 1 avenue de la Madone and 36 rue Comte Félix Gastaldi. These boutiques were established by Princess Grace to provide an outlet for Monégasque products (everything from linens to dolls). Some products are created at workshops here. The profits all go to the Princess Grace Charitable Foundation.

Charles Garnier, who designed the opulent Paris Opera House, designed the **Casino de Monte Carlo** (*see photo on page 47*) in 1878. Appropriately, there's an opera house inside the casino. The marble atrium with 28 Ionic columns welcomes you (for free). The **Salle Garnier**

MONACO HAPPENINGS

The **Printemps des Arts** (Spring Arts Festival) featuring symphonic, opera and ballet performances is held each April to mid-May. The **Monte Carlo Tennis Tournament** is held at the same time. Two major auto races are held in Monaco: The famous **Grand Prix de Monaco** takes place in mid-May, and **Le Rallye** take place in January. Each June, Monte Carlo hosts the **Le Festival International de la Télévision** (International Festival of Television), the television version of the Cannes Film Festival.

(named after the architect) is a red-and-gold, opulent concert hall with an 18-ton chandelier. The **Salon Blanc** has painted muses. Perhaps the most interesting room is the **Salon Rose** (the smoking room). Its ceiling is decorated with cigar-smoking female nudes. Roulette is played in both the **Salle Européen**, with its eight gigantic chandeliers, and in the ornate **Renaissance Hall**. The private rooms (**Salles Privées**) are where high rollers gamble surrounded by carved mahogany. The **Salle Américaine** (free admission) opens early (at noon) and has Las Vegas-style slot machines. It's without a doubt the world's most glamorous casino.

Outside are immaculately maintained gardens, and, in front of the casino, the Art Deco **Café de Paris** where you can sip a pricey mimosa or enjoy a crêpe Suzette. *Info: place du Casino. Tel. 377/92.16.20.00. Open daily for gaming after 2pm. Admission: €10 to the Salle Européen. Additional (at least) €10 to the private backrooms (jacket and tie required in the backrooms. Passport required for entry.) www.casinomontecarlo.com.*

You don't have to pay to get into the **Sun Casino** in the Monte Carlo Grand Hotel.

BEST SLEEPS AND EATS

Hôtel de Paris €€€
You'll be dazzled by the magnificent domed entrance (*see photo on previous page*). The palatial lobby is a masterpiece of stained glass, statues, crystal chandeliers and marble pillars, and the rooms and service match the elegance of the common areas. *Info: place du Casino (opposite the casino). www.montecarloresort.com. Tel. 377/98.06.30.00. V,*

MC, AE. Restaurant, bar, AC, TV, telephone, minibar, in-room safe, hair-dryer, WiFi.

Hôtel Ambassador €-€€
Not everyone can afford to stay at the glamorous Hôtel de Paris or the other exclusive hotels here, and it's not easy to find affordable hotels in this glitzy place. But, this 35-unit hotel has comfortable, if not small, rooms in the Condamine district. *Info: 25 Ave. Prince Pierre. www.ambassadormonaco.com. Tel.377/97.97.96.96. V, MC, AE. Bar, AC, TV, telephone, , WiFi.*

Le Louis XV- Alain Ducasse €€€
This restaurant in the luxurious Hôtel de Paris is run by famous chef Alain Ducasse. Innovative French and Italian cuisine and attentive service. *Infot place du Casino in the Hôtel de Paris. Tel. 377/98. 06.88.64. Closed Tue and Wed. Open Wed lunch in summer. Reservations required.*

Loga €€
This bistro serving Mediterranean fare will not disappoint. Come here for *barbajuans*, the national dish of Monaco. It's ravioli stuffed with chard and ricotta. Delicious! You can dine inside or on the terrace along the shopping street boulevard des Moulins. *Info: 25 blvd des Moulins. Tel. 377/93.30.87.72. Closed Wed (dinner), Sun, and part of Aug.*

Stars 'n Bars €€
Yearning for a little taste of home? Try this American-style sports bar. *Info: 6 quai Antoine-1er. www.starsnbars.com. Tel. 377/97.97.95.95. Closed Mon from Oct-May.*

THE HILL TOWNS ABOVE MONACO
If you've visited Monaco, you may just want to take it easy in peaceful hill towns. We'll start in **La Turbie**. It's 7 miles (11 km) northeast of Nice (via the Grande Corniche).

There's something very peaceful about La Turbie, located in the hills above the coast. It's not as touristy as nearby Eze, and it certainly is quieter than the coastal towns. The massive Roman monument **La Trophée des Alpes** (The Trophy of the Alps) was built in 6 B.C. to celebrate Augustus Caesar's conquest of the Alps. A small museum near the monument, **Musée du Trophée des Alpes**, describes the history of the monument and its restoration. *Info: Tel. 04/93.41.20.84, closed Mon, admission: €6.*

LA TURBIE BEST SLEEPS & EATS

While in La Turbie, visit **Hostellerie Jérôme**. Here you can dine on local specialties from a Michelin-starred chef (€€€) or for more casual and less expensive dining try the **Café de la Fontaine** next door (€€). Start with *salade de cœurs d'artichauts* (salad featuring artichoke heart) and savor the rich *risotto aux cèpes* (mushroom risotto). You can stay the night at one of five lovely rooms here (€€). *Info: 20 rue Comte de Cessole. www.hostelleriejerome.com. Tel. 04/93.41.18.50. Restaurant closed Mon and Tue. Open daily Jul and Aug. Café: 4 avenue du Général De Gaulle. Tel. 04/93.28.52.70. Open daily.*

After La Turbie, follow the signs to **Peillon**. It's 11 miles (18 km) northeast of Nice.

Peillon is a perched village, but unlike so many of the others, it's **void of touristy boutiques**. Why? It's hard to get to. You may feel like

you've stepped back into medieval times. There's only one gateway into this village of ancient homes with red-tiled roofs. You can visit the Baroque church **Eglise St- Saveur** and **Chapelle des Pénitents Blancs**, a chapel with frescoes of the passion of Christ, dating back to the late 15th century.

Though not as unspoiled as Peillon, nearby **Roquebrune** will allow you to wander in relative peace. It's three miles (five km) west of Menton/three miles (five km) east of Monaco, located along the Grande Corniche. The entire village has been renovated, and its steep alleys and arcaded lanes are filled with galleries, boutiques and souvenir shops. The **castle on the hilltop** is said to be the oldest feudal castle in France, built over 1,000 years ago. You can also visit the 12th-century **Eglise Ste-Marguerite**. The long and narrow street **rue Moncollet** is lined with houses dating back to the Middle Ages. Just outside the village stands the Olivier Millénaire, a thousand-year-old olive tree, said to be the oldest tree in the world.

The **Château de Roquebrune** is the oldest feudal castle in France. It's dominated by two square towers (with fantastic views of the coast). Inside is a museum tracing the castle's history. *Info: rue du Château. Tel. 04/93.35.07.22. Open daily. Admission: €5.*

Cap-Martin, 1 1/2 miles west of Roquebrune, is a wealthy, mostly residential seaside resort.

ROQUEBRUNE BEST SLEEPS & EATS
Les Deux Frères €€
Some of the ten guest rooms at this inn have views of the Mediterranean Sea below. You'll be staying in a converted schoolhouse. The Dutch owners provide a friendly welcome and although the rooms are small, the price is right. *Info: 1 place des Deux Frères. www.lesdeux-freres.com. Tel. 04/93.28.99.00. V, MC, AE. Restaurant, AC, TV.*

The **restaurant** here (€€-€€€) will not disappoint. Excellent French, Italian, and Mediterranean dishes. Try the *carré d'agneau* (rack of lamb). Excellent wine list featuring local producers. *Info: Closed Sun (dinner), Mon, and Tue (lunch).*

Au Grand Inquisiteur €€-€€€
Up a steep stairway on your way to the feudal castle, you'll find this small restaurant in a cellar. Good Provençal cooking with a huge wine list. Try the *noisette de cerf grillé* (grilled venison). Note that sometimes it's closed for lunch. *Info: 18 rue du Château. www.augrandinquisiteur. com. Tel. 04/93.35.05.37. Closed Mon.*

MENTON

Depending on which way you look at it, **Menton** is either at the end or the beginning of the French Riviera. It's five miles (nine km) east of Monaco. Menton doesn't feel very French. This isn't solely because of its location on the Italian border, but also a result of the large number of expatriates who have come to Menton to retire. Its climate is the warmest of all the towns in this book, warm enough to grow citrus fruits, and there's a huge **Fête du Citron** (Lemon Festival) held every February. Legend has it that when Adam and Eve were kicked out of the Garden of Eden, Eve snuck out a lemon and planted it in Menton (because the town reminded her of her former home). There are many lovely gardens in the city. Its long **Promenade du Soleil** (on the **Golfe de la Paix**) runs along a narrow pebble beach and the main costal road. Menton's Old Town, with narrow streets and main street **rue St-Michel**, is on the east side of town. It's sedate, but has much to offer the traveler.

There are several museums worth visiting here.

The **Musée des Beaux-Arts** (a fine-arts museum) contains European paintings from the Renaissance to present day. But the real attraction here are the grounds of the Palais Carnoles. The gardens of this 18th-century palace (once the summer home of the Princess of Monaco) are filled with orange, grapefruit and lemon trees. *Info: 3 avenue de la Madone (in the Palais Carnoles). Tel. 04/93.35.49.71. Closed Tue. Admission: Free.*

The **Musée de Préhistoire Régionale** is dedicated to human evolution. Its highlight is the 30,000-year-old head found in 1884 in nearby caves. *Info: rue Lorédan-Larchey. Tel. 04/93.35.84.64. Open 10am-noon and 2pm-6pm. Closed Tue. Admission: Free.*

The **Musée Jean-Cocteau** (sometimes called the Bastion museum) is devoted to the works of writer and artist Jean-Cocteau. It's located in the Bastion du Port, a 17th-century fortress on the port. Cocteau coordinated the restoration of the fortress. *Info: Vieux Port. Tel. 04/93.57.72.30. Open 10am-noon and 2pm-6pm. Closed Tue. Admission: €4.* A new museum dedicated to Cocteau (*www.museecocteaumenton.fr*) opened in 2011 on the waterfront. Included in the €8 admission price is entry to the Bastion museum. Cocteau also adorned the walls and ceiling of the town hall on place Ardoïno.

If you have time, pop into the **Basilique St-Michel**. The bell tower of this Baroque church can be seen throughout Menton. The richly decorated basilica has a huge 17th-century organ. Nearby is the splendid Chapelle de l'Immaculée-Conception, dating back to the 1600s. *Info: Parvis St-Michel. Open daily. Admission: Free.*

In the Old Town between rue St-Michel and the sea is the beautiful **Marché Couvert** (Covered Market). Cheese, fruits, French breads and Italian specialties can all be found here. *Info: Closed Mon.*

MENTON SLEEPS & EATS
Hôtel Riva €€
Hotel Riva enjoys a great location close to the city center and just opposite the sea. Guests can enjoy the top floor sun deck. There's also a spa at the hotel. You'll be close to the sights of Menton and have easy access to the promenade along the sea (which you can follow all the way to Monaco). *Info. 600 Promenade du Soleil. www.rivahotel.com. Tel. 04/92.10.92.10. , MC, AE. Bar, AC, TV, telephone, WiFi. Parking is available for a fee.*

Cirke €€
This restaurant above the Port of Menton serves Italian, Provençal and French food (especially seafood). The specialty here is *grande friture*, a tasty mix of crispy fried squid, scallops. shrimp, and white fish. Good house wine served by the *pichet* (pitcher). *Info: 1 place Victoria. www. restaurantlecirke.com. Tel. 04/89.74.20.54. Open daily.*

VENTIMIGLIA, ITALY
Much of the French Riviera was part of Italy until 1860, so you'll see the Italian influence in everything from architecture to cuisine.

Just across the border from Menton is the Italian town of **Ventimiglia** (Vintimille in French). Why not head here for lunch, so when you return from your trip, you can tell friends that you had lunch in Italy? It has a lovely **Città Vecchia** (Old Town), an 11th-century **Duomo** (cathedral), and many restaurants to choose from. Be warned that traffic can be chaotic on Fridays when there's a vast **mercato** (market) selling everything from flowers to leather goods.

Head to the seafront where you'll have your pick of places to eat pasta and seafood.

What a great way to end your trip to the Riviera!

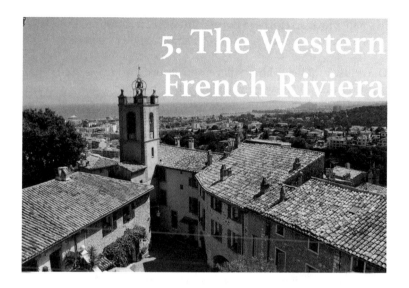

5. The Western French Riviera

HIGHLIGHTS
- A St-Tropez tan and glamorous Cannes

- The ancient town of Antibes

- The incredible clifftop village of Gourdon

- St-Paul-de-Vence, the most visited village in France

INTRO

The **Côte d'Azur** got its name from a guidebook written in 1887 covering the area from the Italian border to Hyères. The author was referring to the coast's clear blue skies, not, as many think, to the blue waters of the Mediterranean Sea. Most English speakers call this area the French Riviera. Hilltop villages, art museums, coastal resorts and a St-Tropez tan all await you in the **western French Riviera**.

If you can, visit after the high-season onslaught of tourists in July and August. It's easier to drive on the *corniches* and easier to park in the small villages. The temperatures are comfortable, and life, especially in smaller towns, returns to normal. In some areas, especially seaside resorts, many places close during November and December.

Once just a quiet fishing village and favorite of artists, **St-Tropez** burst on the world scene when sexy Brigitte Bardot arrived in her sunglasses and capri pants to star in the 1950s film *And God Created Woman*. Despite its reputation as a tourist mecca for the beautiful, rich and famous, it still retains much of its charm. Nearby, you'll find picturesque villages and great beaches in places like **Grimaud, Antibes**, and **Cannes**.

COORDINATES
The **western French Riviera** is in the south of France and stretches **from Nice to St-Tropez**. The area is about 600 miles (966km) south of Paris. From Nice, there is frequent bus service to Antibes and Cannes (#200), St-Paul-de-Vence and Vence (#400), and Grasse (#500). Train service from Nice includes Cannes (40 minutes) and Marseille (2 ½ hours). Most other destinations in Provence require a transfer in Marseille (including to Cassis, Aix, and Avignon).

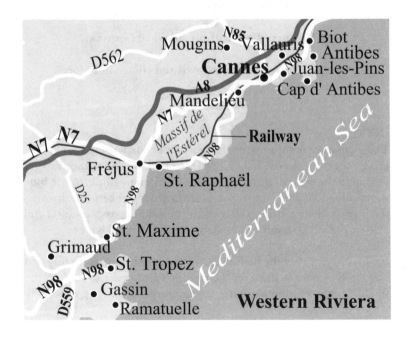

ST-TROPEZ

Let's get a tan in **St-Tropez**. It's 41 miles (66 km) northeast of Toulon/22 miles (35 km) southwest of Fréjus/47 miles (76 km) southwest of Cannes.

Come here to sit in the **Vieux Port** (Old Port) along the quai Jean-Jaurès, where yachts from all over the world dock, and enjoy some of the world's best people-watching. St-Tropez's web of narrow streets in the **Quartier de la Ponche** (Old Town) are lined with pastel-painted buildings with red-tile roofs filled with restaurants and boutiques for

every budget (especially those with an unlimited budget). You can't miss the bell tower of **Eglise St-Tropez**, painted in yellow and orange. Oh, and for that St-Tropez tan, there are some great beaches here, too!

Head for the **Place des Lices** along boulevard Vasserot. Cafés shaded by plane trees line this market square. On Tuesday and Saturday mornings, it's filled with stalls selling everything from produce to antiques. In the evening, you can witness the evening promenade, where locals walk and greet each other.

There's one museum that's a must-see when you want to take a break from shopping and the beaches: the **Musée de l'Annonciade/Musée St-Tropez**. This 14th-century chapel is now a wonderful art museum. You'll find a superb collection of Impressionist and Post-Impressionist paintings by Signac, Matisse and Dufy, to name a few. What makes this museum interesting is that many of the paintings are actually of St-Tropez. *Info: place Grammont (near the Old Port). Tel. 04/94.17.84.10. Open 10am-1pm and 2pm-6pm. Closed Tue. and Nov. Admission: €6.*

You may want to visit the **Citadelle**, where 17th-century ramparts surround this fort. Come here to take in the view of the town and coast and enjoy the quiet park. *Info: rue de la Citadelle.*

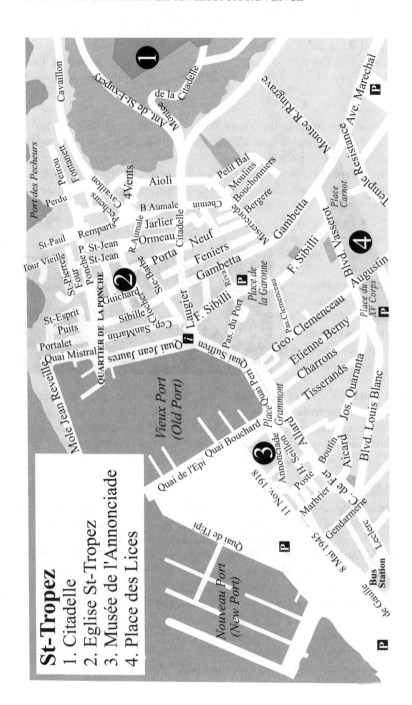

St-Tropez
1. Citadelle
2. Eglise St-Tropez
3. Musée de l'Annonciade
4. Place des Lices

It's the sun and beaches (*les plages*) that attract many visitors to St-Tropez. **Plage de la Bouillabaisse** (don't you love that name?) and **plage des Graniers** are closest to town, accessible by foot and popular with families.

The **Route des Plages** (Beach Road) takes you to some of the best beaches that begin 2 1/2 miles (4 km) south of town at the plage des Salins, accessible by bicycle or car. **Plage des Tahiti** (*photo at right*) is a favorite with nudists, and **Coco Beach** (toward Rama

tuelle) is popular with gays. You'll find bars, restaurants and shops at popular and packed **plage de Pampelonne**. A simple beach seafood restaurant? Ask one of the many celebrities that have stopped at **Le Club 55** on place de Pampelonne.

BEST SLEEPS & EATS
Le Byblos €€€
Trying to get into one of the 52 rooms or 43 suites at this hotel can be a challenge (almost as hard as getting into its Caves du Roy nightclub). If you manage to get in, you'll share the place with celebrities and guests on expense accounts. Modern, comfortable and glamorous. There are two restaurants, both highly acclaimed and expensive: **Restaurant Le "B"** (*Tel. 04/94.56.68.19*) and **Rivea** (*27 ave. Foch. Tel. 04/94.56.68.20*). *Info: Ave. Paul-Signac. www.byblos.com. Tel. 04/94.56.68.00. V, MC, DC, AE. Restaurants, bar, outdoor pool, AC, cable TV, telephone, gym, minibar, hairdryer, safe, WiFi. Closed mid-Oct to Easter.*

Hôtel Le Yaca €€€
This former private home was built in 1722. It was once the meeting place of Impressionist painters such as Paul Signac. The 28-room hotel is situated on a small street in the Old Town. Many of the rooms have views of the beautiful inner flower garden. Upper-floor rooms

have views of the Gulf of St-Tropez. In July and August, there's a shuttle service to the beach (or you can just hang out at the beautiful swimming pool). *Info: 1 blvd. D'Aumale. www.hotel-le-yaca.fr. Tel. 04/94.55.81.00. V, MC, DC, AE. Restaurant, bar, outdoor pool, AC, TV, telephone, minibar, hairdryer, safe, WiFi. Closed mid-Oct to mid-Apr.*

Hôtel Sube €€
Located on the port near the tourist office, this hotel has a lovely lounge and comfortable rooms (you'll pay more for a port view). Great location for shopping. *Info: 15 quai Suffren. Tel. 04/94.97.30.04. www.hotel-sube.com. V, MC, AE. Bar, AC, TV, telephone.*

Lou Cagnard €-€€
This 19-room hotel is located in a renovated villa. It's family-owned and you'll have a warm welcome. Good central location. There's a lovely garden surrounded by fig trees where you can relax or have breakfast for €11. Note that a few of the rooms do not have air conditioning. *Info: 18 ave. Paul-Poussel. www.hotel-lou-cagnard.com. Tel. 04/94.97.04.24. V, MC. AC, TV, telephone, safe, free parking. Closed Nov-Feb.*

L'Aventure €€-€€€
Located on a backstreet, this cozy and unpretentious restaurant will provide better value than those of the same price at the port. Market-fresh French, Mediterranean, and Provençal cuisine is served by a welcoming staff. Try the garlicky *escargot* (snails) and wash it down with one of the local wines offered. *Info: 4 rue du Portail-Neuf. Tel. 04/94.97.44.01. No lunch. Dinner Tue-Sun. Closed Mon.*

Le Girelier €€-€€€
Grilled fish is the specialty at this restaurant on the port. Try the *saumon à la plancha* (grilled salmon). *Info: quai Jean-Jaurès (on the harbor). www.legirelier.fr. Tel. 04/94.97.03.87. Closed mid-Nov to mid-Dec.*

Le Club 55 €€
A simple beachside seafood restaurant? Ask one of the celebrities that have eaten here. There's also a great shop selling everything you need for the beach. *Info: 55 boulevard Patch. plage de Pampelonne. Tel. 04/94.55.55.55.*

Le Magnan €€
Ten minutes from St-Tropez in Cogolin, this restaurant specializes in Provençal country cooking and is located on a hilltop farm. Try the epaule d'agneau confite 7 heures (shoulder of lamb cooked seven hours). Definitely worth the drive. *Info: On route N98 in Cogolin (6 miles (9 km) west of St-Tropez). Tel. 04/94.49.57.54. Closed mid-Oct to Mar.*

BEST NIGHTLIFE & ENTERTAINMENT
VIP Room
Deep pockets? Well dressed? Ready to party? Head to this club where you'll spend at least €20 for a cocktail. But, maybe you'll see Paris Hilton. *Info: Residence du Nouveau Port. www.viproom.com. Tel. 06/38.83.83.83.*

Les Caves du Roy
If you can get in, you can drink and dance the night away at this bar/club in the Byblos Hotel. *Info: Ave. Paul-Signac. www.lescavesduroy.com. Tel. 04/94.56.68.00. Open weekends Apr-Oct. Open nightly Jul and Aug.*

Le Pigeonnier
Fun, fabulous, and gay. If you're straight, you can come here, too. *Info: 19 rue de la Ponche. Tel. 06/33.58.92.45.*

BEST SHOPPING
Jacqueline Thienot
Interesting antiques from throughout the French Riviera. *Info: 2 rue Georges-Clemenceau. Tel. 04/94.97.05.70. Closed Sun.*

Kiwi
Sexy beach wear. *Info: 34 rue Allard. Tel 04/94.97.42.26*

Pause-Douceur
Fantastic French chocolates. *Info: 11 rue Allard, Tel. 04/94.97.27.58.*

Galeries Tropéziennes
Unusual gifts and clothes to bring home. Known for their selection of purses. *Info: 56 rue Gambetta, Tel. 04/94.97.02.21.*

Blanc D'Ivoire/La Maison des Lices
Provençal furniture, linens and household goods. *Info: 18 boulevard Louis-Blanc, Tel. 04/94.97.11.34.*

Reminiscence
Funky jewelry. place la Garonne. *Info: Tel. 04/94.97.21.57.*

AROUND THE GULF OF ST-TROPEZ
While St-Tropez is fabulous, don't ignore the area around it. We'll visit nearby gulf towns and picturesque villages (especially Grimaud). There's something for families, those looking for beach resorts, or those who want to spend their days on the golf course.

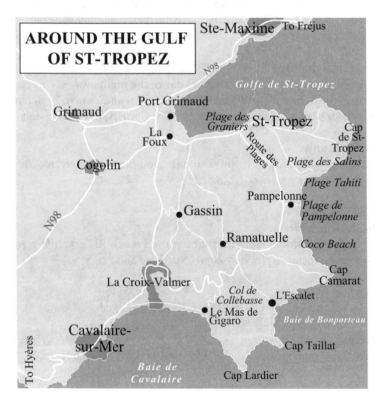

For families, head to **Ste-Maxime**, 7 miles (12 km) east of St-Tropez. This modern resort town directly on the Gulf of St-Tropez (across from St-Tropez) is sheltered by the Maures Mountains. The town is popular with families, and overall is much cheaper than glitzy St-Tropez. There's a large waterfront promenade and a small Old Town. You can view the **Eglise Ste-Maxime**, a 15th-century church, and the **Tour Carrée des Dames** (Dames Tower), a 16th-century tower that houses a museum dedicated to local history. Befitting a resort town, there's also a casino here. Along the casino is the plage du Casino. The large sandy beach **la plage de la Nartelle** is west of town.

If you're interested in visiting a picturesque village, head to **Grimaud**, 6 miles (10 km) west of St-Tropez. This picturesque village is one of France's "Villes Fleuries" (Flowered Villages) and it's truly lovely. The castle ruins (parts dating back to the 11th century) are high above the village and provide excellent vistas of St-Tropez Bay. During the day the town is filled with tourists, but at night it's a quiet place to dine and stroll. The car-free town of **Port Grimaud** (*photo below*) on the coast was constructed in the 1960s as a private resort complete with canals. Sort of a 1960s Venice in the South of France.

For great views of the Bay of Pampelonne, head to **Ramatuelle**, 7 miles (12km) southwest of St-Tropez. Ramatuelle is built into the hills above the Bay of Pampelonne. It's surrounded by vineyards, and the village is enclosed by ramparts. Ancient stone houses line the narrow streets filled with boutiques and souvenir shops for the many day-trippers from St-Tropez. Lots of restaurants and small hotels.

Four miles (seven km) north of Ramatuelle is **Gassin**, another village worth a visit. Gassin is perched high up on a rock surrounded by vineyards. It's less commercial than nearby Ramatuelle. The village has ancient homes and winding streets. Its location is really the reason to visit. Not only can you see the Gulf of St-Tropez, but on a clear day, your view extends over the Maures Mountains.

If beach resorts are more to your liking, the area around the Gulf of St-Tropez offers many opportunities. **Fréjus** is 20 miles (34 km) northeast of St-Tropez. Fréjus and nearby St-Raphaël seem to blend into each other as commercial beach resorts. Despite the town's bikini-wearing image, Fréjus's **Vieille Ville** (Old Town) has important Roman sights. The town was founded in 49 B.C. by Julius Caesar. You can view the remains of the **Théâtre Antique**, the 12,000-seat **Arènes** (an arena used today for the occasional bullfight and concert), and remaining arches of an **aqueduct**. Take a break from your tanning and visit these ruins.

Cité Épiscopale is an impressive fortified group of religious buildings in the Old Town. Outside the entry to the 12th-century cathedral is an octagonal baptistery from a 5th-century church that was located here. The cloisters feature galleries decorated with paintings from the 14th century. There's also a small archeology museum of Roman finds from the surrounding area. *Info: 58 rue de Fleury (in the Old Town). Tel. 04/94.52.14.01. Cloister, baptistery and museum are open Jun-Sep daily 10am-12:30pm and 1:45pm-6:30pm. Oct-May Tue-Sun 10am-1pm and 2pm-5pm. Closed Mon. Cathedral is open daily 8:30am-noon and 2pm-6pm. Admission: Free (cathedral). Cloister, baptistery and museum: €5.50*

FRÉJUS SLEEPS & EATS

L'Amandier €€
In a town filled with restaurants and cafés catering to beachgoers, this restaurant away from the beach serves French and Provençal dishes. The €28 dinner menu is a great value. Delcious *canette rôti* (roasted duck). *Info: 19 rue Desaugiers (in the Old Town). www.restaurant-lamandier.com. Tel. 04/94.53.48.77. Closed Sun, Mon (lunch), and Wed (lunch).*

La Bastide du Clos des Roses €€€
This lovely hotel with seven rooms is located three miles outside of Fréjus. Rooms are lovely and modern bathrooms add to the comfort level here. The heated pool is located along its vineyard. You can sample wine from the vineyard on your terrace. There's a small chapel on the grounds and this is a popular destination for weddings and parties on the weekend. *Info: Located north of Fréjus, route D37 at 1609 Route de Malpasse. www.closdesroses.com. Tel. 04/94.53.32.21. V, MC. Bar, spa, AC, TV, hairdryer, safe, WiFi.*

The restaurant here serves French cuisine in a lovely and comfortable setting with both indoor and outdoor seating. The wine featured here is from its own vineyard. Menus begin at €28. (€€-€€€).

Merging with Fréjus, **St-Raphaël** (1/2 mile [one km] southeast of Fréjus) is a modern beach resort. Unlike its neighbor, it has few historic sights. The **Vieille Ville** (Old Town) is the site of two churches, the 19th-century **Notre-Dame de la Victoire** and the 12th-century **Eglise des Templiers**. Beside the Eglise des Templiers is the Musée d'Archéologie Sous-Marine, a museum dedicated to underwater archeology. *Info: rue des Templiers. Tel. 04/94.19.25.75. Open Tue-Sat 9am-noon and 2pm-6pm. Closed Sun and Mon. Admission: Free.*

You'll find a casino, hotels, and a promenade along the seafront. There are also five golf courses near St-Raphaël.

First and foremost, this town is a beach town. Closest to town is **plage du Veillat**. A five-minute walk east of town is **plage Beau Rivage**. Even further east (about five miles) is **plage du Débarquement**. It was at this beach that the Allies landed in August of 1944 to begin their quest to liberate occupied France in World War II. In the other direction, about six miles west of town, is **plage de St-Ayguls**, a nude beach.

For stunning scenery, drive through the **Massif de l'Estérel** (see photo below) **from St-Raphaël to La Napoule**. This barren area of red volcanic rock provides strange and dramatic views. You can either travel north on route N7 or (for the more adventurous) along the coast on the **Corniche de l'Estérel** (route N98).

Looking for **golf** courses? Then visit **Mandelieu/La Napoule-Plage**. It's 5 miles (8 km) southwest of Cannes/20 miles (32 km) northeast of St- Raphaël. La Napoule is surrounded by the large resort town of **Mandelieu**. It was once a small fishing village on the Golfe de la Napoule. Its main sight is its **château**, a 14th-century fortress on the port. It was converted to a strange and interesting castle by eccentric American sculptor Henry Clews in the early 1900s. Now it's a museum of his works. *Info: Tel. 04/93.49.95.05. www.chateau-lanapoule.com. Open Feb-Oct 10am-6pm (three guided tours daily). Nov-Jan Mon-Fri 2pm-6pm (two guided tours daily), Sat and Sun 10am-5pm (three guided tours daily). Admission: €6.*

CANNES

Get glamorous in **Cannes**. It's 20 miles (33 km) southwest of Nice/45 miles (73 km) northeast of St-Tropez. You can reach Cannes from Nice by bus (#200, 1 3/4 hours) and by train (40 minutes).

This alluring resort with nearly perfect weather is best known for its **Festival International du Film** (international film festival) held every May, hosting countless film stars, over 4,000 journalists, and 1,500 other members of the media from around the world.

Head to **La Croisette**, a two-mile promenade on the waterfront. You'll see palm trees, polished yachts from every imaginable place in the world, incredible shops, ultra-luxury hotels and some of the most interesting sun-worshippers in the world.

At the beginning of La Croisette is the **Palais des Festivals** (Festivals

Palace)/**Allée des Etoiles** (Walk of the Stars). Nicknamed "the bunker," the modern Palais des Festivals is the venue for the International Film Festival and many other events. Over 300 handprints are set in concrete on the Walk of Stars surrounding the Festival Hall. Also here is the Casino Croisette.

At number 47 La Croisette is **Malmaison**. This 19th-century mansion hosts changing photography and modern-art exhibits. *Info: 47 La Croisette. Tel. 04/97.06.44.90. Admission: Depends on the exhibit.*

Just north of the Festivals Palace is **Notre-Dame de Bon Voyage**, a 19th-century Gothic-style church, where you can pray that you won't lose all your money at the nearby casinos. *Info: Square Mérimée. Open daily. Admission: Free.*

If you're looking for a place to take a break, there are plenty of cafés and restaurants along the waterfront.

Le Suquet (Old Town) is on a hill on the west end of town. Narrow passageways lead to the **Tour du Suquet**, a 14th-century tower. *Info: Up rue St-Antoine from the waterfront (above quai St-Pierre).*

In the Old Town on the place de la Castre is **Notre-Dame de l'Espérance,** a 16th -century Gothic church, *Info: place de la Castre. Open daily. Admission: Free.*

At the top of Old Town is the **Musée de la Castre**. This museum is ambitious. It has a section on Mediterranean antiquities, a section of 19th-century paintings, and a section with sculpture, paintings and decorative arts from all over the world. *Info: In the Château de la Castre at the top of La Suquet. Tel. 04/93.38.55.26. Closed Mon. Daily Jul and Aug. Admission: €6.50.*

If you're into shopping, there's something for everyone here. A few highlights of the phenomenal shopping in Cannes are:

• **Le Marché Forville** a covered market not too far from Festival Hall featuring a flea market (Mon) and a produce and flower market (Tue through Sun)

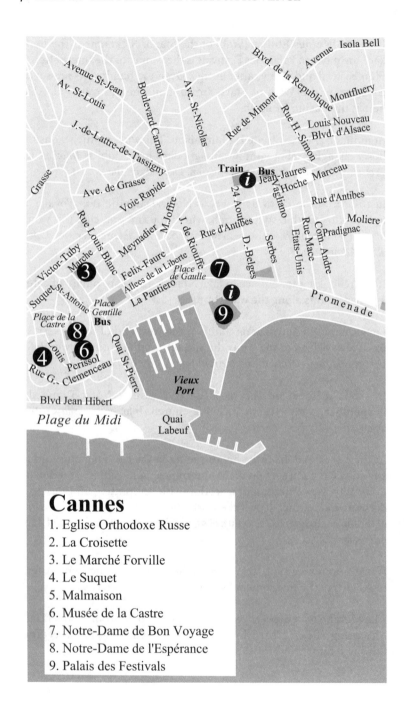

Cannes

1. Eglise Orthodoxe Russe
2. La Croisette
3. Le Marché Forville
4. Le Suquet
5. Malmaison
6. Musée de la Castre
7. Notre-Dame de Bon Voyage
8. Notre-Dame de l'Espérance
9. Palais des Festivals

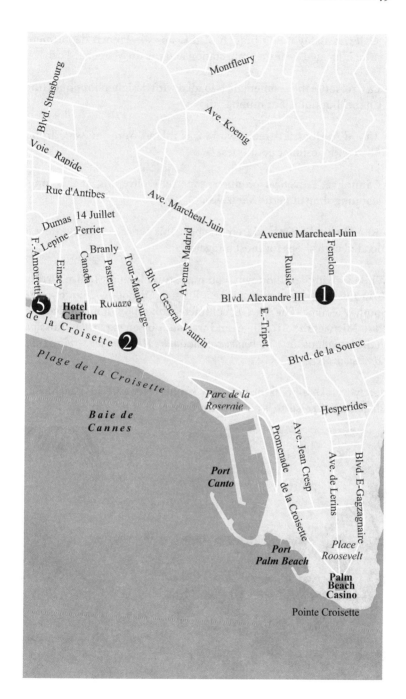

- **Galeries Lafayette:** a branch of this upscale French department store is located near the train station at 6 rue du Maréchal-Foch

- **La Croisette:** the promenade is loaded with designer boutiques (the Chanel boutique is at number 5!)

- **Rue d'Antibes:** a street (two blocks inland from the waterfront) filled with designer boutiques

- **Cannolive:** Provençal products, especially olive oils, at this long-standing shop at 16 rue Vénizelos.

- **Rue Meynadier:** inland from the port, this pedestrian-only street is loaded with shops for most budgets

While walking around town, you may stumble upon **Eglise Orthodoxe Russe.** It's so strange to see a Russian Orthodox Church in the South of France. The church, complete with onion dome, is dedicated to Michael the Archangel and was built by an expatriate Russian in the late 1800s. *Info: 40 boulevard Alexandre III. Open for services only. Admission: Free.*

Ready to take a break or just be a voyeur? Head to the beach! The **Plage de la Croisette** is along the promenade of the same name.

For the most part, this is not a public beach. You must pay a fee (beginning at about €20) for use of a chaise longue, access to showers, food and drink service, an umbrella, and other amenities.

For **free beaches**, try **plage Gazagnaire** to the east, or **plage du Midi** to the west.

Off the coast of Cannes are the **Iles de Lérins**. Traffic-free and tranquil, these islands can be reached by ferry from the Old Port (€15). It takes 15 minutes to get to **Ile Ste-Marguerite** (filled with pine and eucalyptus trees, it's home to Fort Royal, where "The Man in the Iron Mask" was imprisoned); and 30 minutes to **Ile St-Honorat** (home to a fortified abbey).

If you're interested in abstract art, you can visit the **Espace de l'Art Concret** outside of Cannes in Mouans-Sartoux (in the castle), which houses a collection of 350 abstract works. *Info: www.espacedelartconcret.fr. Tel. 04/93.75.71.50. Open Sep-Jun Tue-Sun 1pm 6pm. Closed Mon. Jul and Aug daily 11am-7pm. Admission: €7.*

Golfers flock to the area around Cannes. Five miles (eight km) northeast of Cannes on route D35 is the **Golf Club de Cannes-Mandelieu**, where golfers can enjoy two stunning golf courses (18 holes and 9 holes). *Info: www.golfoldcourse.com. Tel. 04/92.97.32.00. Open daily.*

CANNES SLEEPS & EATS
InterContinental Carlton €€€
The hotel in Cannes (and has been for years). Fashionable, plush and filled with celebrities during the film festival. Scenes from the Cary Grant and Grace Kelly movie *To Catch a Thief* were filmed here. Every amenity imaginable. Fantastic waterfront location with its own private beach. *Info: 58 blvd. De la Croisette. www.intercontinental-carlton-cannes.com. Tel. 04/93.06.40.06. V, MC, DC, AE. Restaurant, bar, gym, room service, AC, TV, telephone, CD player, minibar, in-room safe, hairdryer, WiFi.*

Hôtel Splendid €€-€€€
We can't all stay at the Carlton, but we can perhaps afford the Splendid (especially in off-season). This 62-room, gleaming white hotel (*see photo on next page*) was renovated a few years ago, and has views over

looking the harbor. *Info: 4-6 rue Félix-Faure. www. splendid-hotel-cannes.fr. Tel. 04/97.06.22.22. V, MC, AE. AC, TV, telephone, Internet, in-room safe, hairdryer, WiFi.*

Hôtel Albert 1er €
Cannes is an expensive place to sleep. This mansion, in a mostly residential neighborhood, has been renovated and provides 12 small, clean, and comfortable rooms. Note that it is located uphill from the port and beaches. A good budget choice as rooms start at around €70. *Info: 68 ave. de Grasse. www.hotel-albert1e-cannes. com. Tel. 04/93.39.24.04. V, MC, AE. AC, TV, WiFi.*

La Mère Besson €€-€€€
Old favorite serving Provençal dishes. Fantastic duck-breast dishes. *Info:13 rue des Frères-Pradignac (a few streets north of the waterfront). Tel. 04/93.39.59.24. Closed Sun. Reservations required.*

La Table du Chef €€€
Unpretentious bistro (in a town of lots of pretentious restaurants) serving innovative French cuisine. There is no written menu, so you'll have to order the fixed menu. Chef Bruno Gensdarme worked at the famous Guy Savoy restaurant in Paris. He shops at local produce markets and then creates a nightly four-course menu for €41. You won't be disappointed. *Info: 5 rue Jean Daumas (off of rue d'Antibes). Tel. 04/93.38.35.86. Closed Sun and Mon. Dinner served Thu-Sat.*

CANNES NIGHTLIFE & ENTERTAINMENT
Head to **rue Félix Faure** where you will find many bars and clubs.

Carlton
The grand hotel bar at the InterContinental Carlton Hotel. Glamorous and expensive. *Info: 58 La Croisette. Tel. 04/93.06.40.06.*

Le Bâoli
Get out your wallet and enjoy cocktails at this restaurant/lounge and

dance bar. *Info: Port Pierre Canto. www.lebaoli.com. Tel. 04/93.39.43.03.43.*

Casino Croisette
Part with your money at this popular casino located in the Palais des Festivals. *Info: 1 espace Lucien Barrière. www.lucienbarriere.com. Tel. 04/92.98.78.00.*

There are several **gay and gay-friendly** establishments in Cannes:

• **Vogue**, *20 rue du Suquet, Tel. 04/93.39.99.18 (bar)*
• **Disco**, *7 rue Rouguiere, Tel. 04/93.39.10.36 (club)*

GOLFING IN THE FRENCH RIVIERA

Terre Blanche Hotel Spa Golf Resort €€€
Golfers will be in heaven at the two 18-hole courses. The resort, just south of Tourrettes and Fayence (19 miles [30 km] from Cannes and 35 miles [56 km] from Nice), offers everything a golf lover or non-golf lover could ever want. *Info: www. scottdunn.com. Tel. 04/94.39.90.00. V, MC, DC, AE. Restaurant, bar, room service, outdoor pool, gym, AC, TV, telephone, CD/DVD player, minibar, hairdryer, safe, WiFi.*

• **Friends**, *52 rue Jean-Jaurés, Tel. 04/94.49.20.50 (club)*
• **Le 9 G**, *8 Ch. De l'Industrie-Le Cannet. Tel. 06/17.94.29.24 (sauna)*.

AROUND CANNES

The area around Cannes offers local-history museums, photography museums, art museums, and perfume museums.

We'll start in **Mougins**, five miles (eight km) north of Cannes. The area around Mougins has become a business center and home to thousands of French and international companies. The old village has been restored, and is filled with flowers and galleries. There's a free **Museum of Local History** in the St-Bernardin Chapel (*Tel. 04/92.28.05.47*) and a **Museum of Photography** (see below). Picasso and other artists came here in the 1960s, and Picasso died here in 1973. His final home is in the priory next door to the **Chapelle Notre-Dame de Vie**, an ancient church overlooking the Bay of Cannes. Note that Picasso's former home is privately owned, and the chapel is only open for services. *Info: It's located off of route D35 (1 mile [1.5 km] south-east of town).*

Behind the Porte Sarassine, a 12th-century gate, the **Musée de la Pho-**

tographie is filled with photography equipment and photos (some of Picasso during his life in Mougins). *Info: At the Porte Sarassine 67 rue de l'Eglise. Tel. 04/93.75.85.67. Closed Mon. and Jan. Admission: Free.*

MOUGINS SLEEPS & EATS
Le Moulin de Mougins €€-€€€
This inn has nine suites/rooms. Most are filled with those dining at the restaurant of the same name, as this is the place to come for a luxurious dinner when staying in Cannes or Mougin. The inn, restaurant and cooking school is in a 16th-century olive mill surrounded by mimosas and palms. If it's good enough for Sharon Stone and Elizabeth Taylor, it should be good enough for you. Acclaimed chef Roger Verfé (who helped promote Provençal cuisine throughout the world) began this restaurant and now Chef Erwan Louaisil serves his innovative dishes here. *Info: Notre-Dame-de-Vie (1 mile southeast of Mougins and 4 miles inland from Cannes). www.moulin-mougins.com. Tel. 04/93.75.78.24. V, MC, DC, AE. TV, AC, minibar, WiFi. Restaurant (€€€) closed January. Reservations required. Hotel closed Nov-Apr.*

Grasse is 10 miles (17 km) northwest of Cannes/14 miles (22 km) northwest of Antibes/26 miles (42 km) southwest of Nice. Once a famous resort destination (the likes of Queen Victoria used to come here), today

Grasse is a modern town and the headquarters of some of the world's best-known and largest perfume manufacturers. The majority of all perfume sold in the world contains essences from Grasse. The city's three largest perfume makers have free guided tours: **Fragonard** at 20 boulevard Fragonard, **Molinard** at 60 boulevard Victor-Hugo, and **Galimard** at 73 route de Cannes (two miles [three km] south of the center of town). Lots of signs point the way to these factories. The **Vieille Ville** (Old Town) has narrow, steep streets without the glitz of coastal old towns.

Grasse has three very different museums. The **Musée International de la Parfumerie** (International Perfume Museum) will tell you everything you wanted to know about perfume and its 4,000-year history. Put your nose to the test at one exhibit by trying to identify different fragrances. *Info: 2 blvd du Jue de Ballon. Tel. 04/97.05.58.00. Closed Tue from Ocr-Mar. Closed part of Nov. Admission: €4. There are lovely gardens here that are open from Apr-Nov. Admission: €3.*

Another museum is the **Musée Fragonard**. Fragonard was one of France's distinguished 18th-century artists. This museum honors this native son of Grasse and showcases his paintings. *Info: 23 boulevard Fragonard. Tel. 04/93.36.52.98. Closed Tue from Ocr-Mar. Closed part of Nov. Admission: €4. Currently closed for renovations.*

You'll find local paintings, archeological finds, household items and pottery at the **Musée d'Art et d'Histoire de Provence** (Museum of Art and History of Provence). *Info: 2 rue Mirabeau. Tel. 04/93.36.80.20. Closed Tue from Ocr-Mar. Closed part of Nov. Admission: Free.*

GRASSE SLEEPS & EATS
La Bastide St-Antoine €€€
A 200-year-old farmhouse and inn (the Rolling Stones once stayed here) is the site of an award-winning restaurant (€€€). There are nine luxury rooms and seven suites. *Info: 48 avenue Henri-Dunant. www.jacques-chibois.com. Tel. 04/93.70.94.94. V, MC, DC, AE. AC, TV, telephone, minibar, in-room safe, hairdryer, WiFi.*

If you're up for more touring, you can visit **Vallauris/Golfe-Juan**. It's four miles (six km) west of Antibes/four miles (six km) northeast of Cannes.

Vallauris is a working-class-town and has long been a center for the production of **pottery and ceramics**. Most come here to visit the museum dedicated to the works of Picasso. On the coast is the port of Golfe-Juan. It was here in 1815 that Napoléon arrived after being exiled to the island of Elba in his attempt to return to power. Today it's a family beach resort.

Picasso lived in this town in the 1940s and devoted much of his time to creating pottery. The **Musée National Picasso** (La Guerre et La Paix) is located in the 16th-century Château de Vallauris. Two of Picasso's paintings (*La Paix* [Peace] and *La Guerre* [War]) decorate three of the walls. Also here are the **Musée de la Céramique Moderne**, exhibiting Picasso and others' ceramic works, and **Musée Magnelli**, devoted to the works of Italian abstract artist Alberto Magnelli. *Info: place de la Libération. Tel. 04/93.64.71.83. Closed Tue. Admission: €4.*

If you'd like to take a detour from the coast and its resorts, you can drive 110 miles (176 km) along the **Route Napoléon** from Grasse (near the coast) to Sisteron, mainly on route N85. Napoléon Bonaparte abdicated in April, 1814, and fled to the island of Elba. Nearly a year later, he landed near Cannes. From Cannes, Napoléon and 1,200 men followed small trails and mule tracks through the hills. Traveling its entirety can take up to 15 hours.

Plaques commemorating his return are found all along this panoramic drive. **Sisteron** is the northern gateway to Provence. It's crowned by a 14th-century fortified citadel. On your way up to the citadel is the 12th-century church of **Notre-Dame des Pommiers**. You'll find incredible views of the Durance River valley from the citadel after you climb up Sisteron's tiny winding streets, covered alleys and steep stairways. The last inhabitants of the citadel were the Nazis in 1944, who used it as a prison and military base.

ANTIBES
Antibes is an ancient town with 17th-century ramparts and a fortress wall dropping into the sea. It's 9 miles (15 km) southeast of Nice/7 miles (11 km) northeast of Cannes. You can reach Antibes from Nice by bus (#200, 1.5 hours) and by train (30 minutes).

The streets of its **Vieil Antibes** (Old Town) are lined with Italianate buildings with red-tile roofs. High over the water is the medieval castle, the **Château Grimaldi**. It's also a major tourist destination, with a sandy beach, boutiques and cafés. **Port Vauban Harbor** is packed with some of the largest yachts in the world.

Begin your visit in Antibes at the harborside car park along **avenue de Verdun** (the main street along the harbor).

Pass through the **Porte Marine** (arched gateway). The rampart walls date back to the 17th century when Antibes was the last town before the Italian border. You'll now be in the **Vieil Antibes** (Old Town) on rue Aubernon lined with Italianate buildings.

If you're looking to take a break at a café, head to the tree-lined **Place Nationale** on rue de la République.

The heart of Antibes is the 19th-century canopy of the **Marché Provençal** (Provence Market). Everything from flowers to produce to crafts to beachwear can be found here.

Regional products are sold at **Balade en Provence**, a small shop along the covered market. You should go downstairs where there is a good selection of regional wines, absinthe, and a tasting room. *Info: 25 cours Massena. Tel. 04/93.34.93.00.*

In the Old Town, at place de la Cathédrale, is the **Eglise de l'Immaculée-Conception** (Church of the Immaculate Conception). Its bell tower dates back to the 11th century. Inside you can view its Baroque painted altars.

Across the street from the cathedral is the famous **Musée Picasso**. Picasso spent a very productive year here in the early 1940s at the Château Grimaldi. He gave the museum 300 works (ceramics, drawings, paintings, lithographs, tapestries, sculptures, and oils on paper). There are works by other artists, too, including Miró and Calder. *Info: place du Château (in the Château Grimaldi). Tel. 04/92.90.54.20. Open Tue-Sun mid-Sep to mid-Jun 10am-noon and 2pm-6pm, mid-Jun to mid-Sep 10am-6pm. Closed Mon. Admission: €6.*

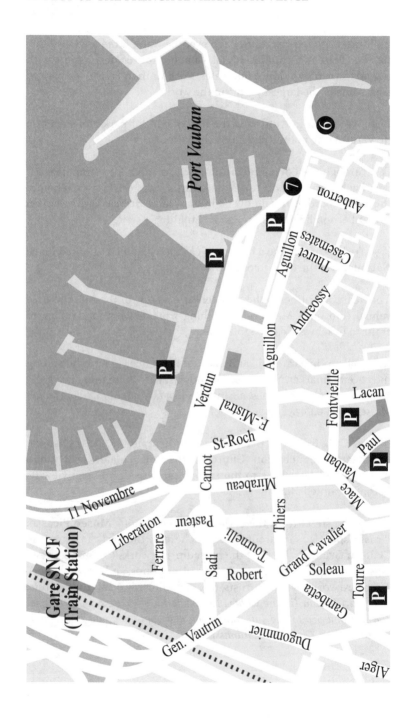

Antibes

1. Eglise de l'Immaculée-
   Conception
2. Marché Provençal
3. Musée d'Histoire et
   d'Archéologie
4. Musée Picasso
5. Place Nationale
6. Plage de la Gravette
7. Porte Marine

 If you're interested in catching some rays, join the sunbathers at the public beach, **plage de la Gravette.**

The archeology museum **Musée d'Histoire et d'Archéologie** is located in the fortress Bastion-St-André. It's filled with finds from the area dating back to the Greeks, who settled here in the 4th-century B.C. *Info: Tel. 04/93.95.85.98. Open Tue-Sun 10am-noon and 2pm-6pm. Closed Mon. Admission: €3.*

Whales, sharks, dolphins, sea lions, waterslides, miniature golf, petting zoo...you get the picture. Children will love **Marineland.** *Info: On route N7 2 miles (4 km) east of town. www.marineland.fr. Tel. 04/93.33.49.49. Closed Oct-Dec but otherwise open daily at 10am. Admission: €45 adults, €36 children (under 13).*

You may want to spend some time in **Cap d' Antibes,** just one mile (two km) south of Antibes. Since the 19th century, this peninsula has been home to luxury villas shaded by massive pines and protected by privacy gates.

One of the world's most glamorous hotels (**Hôtel du Cap-Eden Roc**) is located here. There are fabulous views from the **Phare de la Garoupe** (lighthouse) next to the 16th-century chapel of Notre-Dame-de-la-Garoupe.

If you're interested in subtropical plants and trees, head to the **Jardin Thuret.** Thuret was the man responsible for introducing the palm tree to this area. *Info: boulevard du Cap. Tel. 04/97.21.25.00. Open 8am-6pm. Closed weekends. Admission: Free.*

ANTIBES/CAP D'ANTIBES SLEEPS & EATS
Hôtel du Cap-Eden Roc €€€
Simply one of the world's most glamorous hotels. It's so exclusive that it didn't take credit cards until a few years ago. The swimming pool,

dug into solid rock, is spectacular. It's surrounded by nine acres of lush gardens. *Info: Blvd. J.F.-Kennedy in Cap d'Antibes. www.edenroc-hotel. fr. Tel. 04/93.61.39.01. Restaurant, bar, outdoor pool, tennis courts, AC, TV, telephone, minibar, safe, hairdryer, WiFi.*

Castel Garoupe €€
This hotel is located in a villa in Cap d'Antibes. Attractive pool, flowered gardens and comfortable rooms. Some rooms have a small terrace or balcony. Studios and apartments have kitchenettes. *Info: 959 blvd. de la Garoupe. www.castel-garoupe.com. Tel. 04/93.61.36.51. V, MC, AE. Bar, outdoor pool, gym, AC (some rooms), TV (some rooms), telephone, minibar, safe, hairdryer, WiFi.*

A MEMORABLE SUNSET
Begin this phenomenal walk at the **plage de la Garoupe**, the cape's beach. You can park at the public parking lot. At the end of the beach and parking lot is the **Sentier du Littoral**. This stone path (at times dirt) has steps etched into the rocky coastline. Although it winds its way around the entire cape, remember that you need to return to your car. It's for the adventurous and at times the waves can make the path slippery and dangerous. A memorable walk at sunset!

Hôtel La Jabotte €€
A small gem of a hotel (really more like a bed and breakfast) for the cost, hidden down an alley in Cap d'Antibes. Lovely patio garden, basic accommodations and friendly owners. *Info: 13 ave. Max-Maurey. www.jabotte.com. Tel. 04/93.61.45.89. V, MC. AC, TV, telephone. WiFi available.*

Les Vieux Murs €€€
This candlelit restaurant/tavern is located in a vaulted room inside the town walls near the Musée Picasso. Great views of the sea. Local seafood is the specialty. Large selection of wines from Provence. *Info: 25 promenade Amiral-de-Grasse. www.lesvieuxmurs.com. Tel. 04/93.34.06.73. Sun (in winter).*

Café Milano €-€€
Small, intimate restaurant with an open kitchen. Dishes are beautifully presented. Try one of the excellent Italian dishes offered such

as *risotto aux artichauts et safran* (artichoke and saffron risotto) or *tagliolini aux champignons* (tagliolini pasta with mushrooms). These are some of the vegetarian options, but you can order fish or meat. *Info: 2 rue de la Tourrague (near the intersection of cours Masséna). www.cafemilano-antibes.com. Tel. 04/89.68.62.18. Closed Mon.*

Le Brûlot/ Le Brûlot Pasta €-€€

Crowded, hectic bistro one street inland from the open-air market, serving authentic Provençal fare. Le Brûlot Pasta serves Italian dishes and pizza cooked in a wood oven. *Info: Le Brûlot: 3 rue Frédéric-Isnard (off of rue Clemenceau). Tel. 04/93.34.17.76. Closed Sun (lunch). Le Brûlot Pasta: Tel. 04/93.34.19.19. Open daily for dinner.*

Juan-les-Pins is three miles (five km) southwest of Antibes.

Modern, crowded, sexy and a little bit naughty. Juan-les-Pins, developed in the 1920s, is known for its nightlife and tends to draw a younger crowd than nearby Antibes. You can take a break from visiting the clubs at Eden Casino. While most of the coast has pebble beaches, the town's three public beaches, **plage de Juan-les-Pins, plage de la Salis** and **plage de la Garoupe**, are sandy. It hosts a world-renowned **jazz festival** every July. *Info: www.antibes-juanlespins.com.*

JUAN-LES-PINS SLEEPS & EATS

Le Perroquet €€

The name of the restaurant means "the parakeet" (if you couldn't tell that from its décor). Provençal dishes served in an attractive setting. The house specialty is grilled fish. *Info: avenue Georges-Gallice (across from Parc de la Pinède). Tel. 04/93.61.02.20. Closed mid-Nov to end of Dec.*

AROUND ANTIBES

Pottery, art and unbelievable scenery are in store for you in the area around Antibes. Begin in **Biot**, four miles (six km) northwest of Antibes. This 16th-century hilltop village is known for its pottery, ceramics and glassblowing. Around the main square, the **place des Arcades**, are the ancient gateways and the **Eglise de Biot** with its elaborately decorated 15th-century altar screens.

There are many shops here where you can buy pottery, ceramics and decorative glassware, and most of them are near the place des

Arcades. You can watch glassblowers and purchase expensive glassware at **Verreries de Biot**. *Info: 5 chemin des Combes on the edge of town. Closed part of Jan.*

The **Musée d'Histoire Locale et de Céramique Biotoise** chronicles the importance of ceramics, pottery and glassblowing in local history. *Info: place de la Chapelle/9 rue St-Sébastien. Tel. 04/93.65.54.54. Closed Mon and Tue. Admission: €4.*

You may also want to visit the **Musée National Fernand-Léger** on the east end of the village. Léger was a French cubist painter who died in 1955. This national museum, with its very colorful exterior, houses over 300 of his works. *Info: Chemin du Val de Pome (on the east end of the village). Tel. 04/92.91.50.30. Closed Tue. Admission: €6.*

Next door to the Musée National Fernand-Léger is the **Bonsaï Arboretum** with a collection of over 1,000 bonsai trees, some of which are over 1,000 years old. *Info: 229 chemin du Val de Pome (on the east end of the village). www.museedubonsai-biot.fr. Tel. 04/93.65.63.99. Closed Tue. Admission: €4.*

Inland is the incredible village of **Gourdon**, 9 miles (14 km) north of Grasse.

This clifftop village stands dramatically on limestone overlooking the Loup River Valley. It's worth the drive up the winding roads. The town offers spectacular views (and we do mean spectacular) of both the coast and the river canyon. The Loup River has cut its way through the limestone to create a series of rapids and waterfalls, and the river canyon is one of the most accessible in the area. You can walk from town down the adventurous **chemin du Paradis**. The city is popular with hikers, rafters and trout fishermen. It's an ancient feudal town where you can visit the tranquil gardens of **Gourdon Castle**.

If you want to check out one more village near Antibes, head to the lovely town of **Tourrettes-sur-Loup**. It's 18 miles (29 km) west of Nice/4 miles (6 km) west of Vence.

This village with its three towers sits on a cliff overlooking the Loup River Valley. The walls of the outer buildings of the village also serve as ramparts. It's a center for the cultivation of violets, and you'll see them everywhere. The **Old Town** is lovely and worth a stroll. You can visit the **Chapelle St-Jean** next to **Roman ruins**. The town is loaded with interesting galleries selling their crafts and plenty of candy shops, some of them selling sugar candy made with local violets (we told you they were everywhere).

FURTHER AFIELD

Join the crowds in **St-Paul-de-Vence**, 19 miles (31 km) north of Nice.

Said to be the most visited village in France, St-Paul is crowded with day-trippers from the coastal resort towns and Nice. What makes it so popular is its walled, beautifully preserved **Old Town** of stone houses dating back to the 16th and 17th centuries. You can walk down the car-free **Grande Rue** (main street) past its souvenir shops and art galleries, up to the art-filled **La Collégiale de la Conversion de St-Paul** (an early Gothic church), and visit the **Musée d'Histoire Locale** (Local History Museum).

Outside the town walls on the hilltop (a 15-minute uphill walk from town or access by car) is the **Fondation Maeght**. Even those not interested in modern art can appreciate this world-famous venue. Glass walls let you take in the pine-shaded gardens and terraces while you view changing exhibits of works by such artists as Chagall, Matisse, Kandinsky, Calder, and Miró. This private museum was established in the 1960s by art dealer Aimé Maeght, and its unique architecture alone is worth a visit. *Info: Outside the town walls on the hilltop (a 15-minute uphill walk from town or access by car). www.fondation-maeght.com. Tel. 04/93.32.81.63. Open daily Jul-Sep 10am-7pm. Oct-Jun 10am-6pm. Admission: €15.*

ST-PAUL-DE-VENCE SLEEPS & EATS
Auberge Le Hameau €€-€€€
This former farmhouse on the outskirts of town provides an oh, so Riviera experience. Some of the 17 rooms and suites have terraces facing the lovely outdoor pool; others have views of St-Paul or the

Mediterranean Sea. Rooms are decorated with Provençal furniture. *Info: 528 Route D107 (a little less than 1 mile from St-Paul in the direction of Colle). www.le-hameau.com. Tel. 04/93.32.80.24. V, MC. Bar, outdoor pool, AC, TV, gym, telephone, minibar, hairdryer, safe, WiFi. Closed mid-Nov to mid-Feb.*

La Colombe d'Or €€€
This exclusive, family-run 26-room villa is just 12 miles from Nice, and is surrounded by cypress trees. Beautiful outdoor pool. Cozy rooms decorated with ceramic tile. Most come here for its restaurant, with art of such notables as Picasso and Utrillo on the walls. *Info: 1 place du Général-de-Gaulle. www.la-colombe-dor.com. Tel. 04/93.32.80.02. V, MC, DC, AE. Restaurant, bar, outdoor pool, AC, TV, telephone, minibar, hairdryer, safe, WiFi. Closed Nov and Dec.*

Le Tilleul €€
Located on the town's ramparts, this restaurant is a great place to relax for breakfast, lunch, or dinner. The all-French wine list includes many selections by the glass. Sip your wine while sitting under the large lime tree or dine on modern French cuisine in the attractive indoor dining area. Try the *poulet fermier cuisiné au lait de coco et curry* (free-range chicken in a coconut milk and curry sauce). If you're miss-

ing Mexican beer, they also serve Corona! *Info: place du Tilleul. www. restaurant-letilleul.com. Tel. 04/93.32.80.36. Open daily in season.*

Just two miles (four km) north of St-Paul-de-Vence is the city of **Vence.**

Vence is a modern commercial town and most travelers head to its walled **Cité Historique** (Old Town). Most of the renovated Old Town dates back to the 15th century. Sections of the original walls survive and there are five *portes* (gates) that remain. Inside these gates are the 13th-century watchtower of the **Château de Villeneuve** on **place du Frêne** (which takes its name from the ancient ash tree (*frêne*) here), the **place du Peyra** (with its lovely fountains), and the **place Clemenceau** (dominated by the City Hall). On **place Godeau** is the **Cathédrale de la Nativité de la Vierge** (Cathedral of the Birth of the Virgin), with portions dating back to the 10th century.

On the northern outskirts of town is the **Chapelle du Rosaire** (Chapel of the Rosary). At the age of 77, in thanks to a Dominican nun (and sometimes model!) who nursed him back to health, Matisse designed and decorated this small chapel on the northern outskirts of town. Its white walls are highlighted with blue-and-green stained-glass windows and black-and-white Stations of the Cross. The admission includes entry to a museum that chronicles the design and construction of the chapel. *Info: 466 avenue Henri-Matisse. Tel. 04/93.58.03.26. Open Mon, Wed, and Sat 2pm-5:30pm. Open Tue and Thu 10am-11:30am and 2pm-5:30pm. Closed Fri, Sun (except for mass at 10am) and mid-Nov to mid-Dec. Admission: €5.*

VENCE EATS

La Farigoule €€-€€€
Classic Provençal cuisine with indoor and outdoor dining. The Provençal dish *pissaladière* (a pizza-like tart with onions, black olives and purée of anchovies and sardines) is a specialty here. *Info: 15 rue Henri-Isnard (in the Old Town). www.lafarigoule-vence.fr. Tel. 04/93.58.01.27. Closed Mon and Tue.*

If you're up for more touring, you can visit **Cagnes-sur-Mer,** 4 miles (6 km) south of St-Paul-de-Vence/13 miles (21 km) northeast of Cannes.

Cagnes-sur-Mer is really three different places. At the sea is the former fishing village and now modern beach resort of **Cros-de-Cagnes** (with a pebble beach). Inland is the modern town of **Cagnes-Ville**, and up the hill is the beautiful fortified medieval village of **Haut-de-Cagnes.**

In Haut-de-Cagnes, you'll find the **Château de Cagne**. This Grimaldi fortress was built in the early 1300s. Inside its walls is an elegant palace dating back to 1602. It houses the museum of modern Mediterranean art and a museum dedicated to the history of the olive tree. *Info: place Grimaldi. Tel. 04/93.02.47.35. Closed Tue. Admission: €4.*

Admirers of Renoir should visit the **Musée Renoir**, located in the former home of the artist. It has been renovated and restored to how it was when he died in 1919. The museum sits in the middle of olive groves just east of the Old Town. Eleven of his paintings and the largest collection of his sculpture are here, along with those of his contemporaries. *Info: avenue des Collettes (brown signs mark the way). Tel. 04/93.20.61.07. Open Jun-Sep Wed-Mon 10am-1pm and 2pm-6pm, Oct-Mar 10am-noon and 2pm-5pm, Apr-May 10am-noon and 2pm-6pm. Closed Tue. Admission: €6.*

HAUT-DE-CAGNES SLEEPS & EATS
Le Grimaldi €€
Indoor and outdoor dining on the Old Town square at this family-owned restaurant serving local specialties. Try the *lapin* (rabbit). The small inn (€€) features five comfortable rooms. *Info: 6 place du Château in Haut-de-Cagnes. Tel. 04/93.08.17.12. Open Oct-Mar. Inn: V, MC, AE. TV, AC, WiFi.*

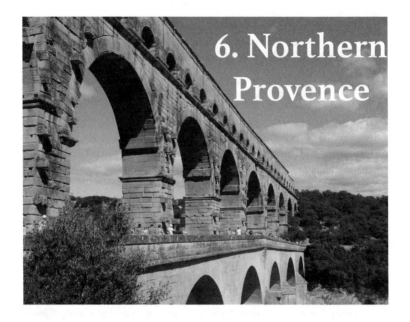

6. Northern Provence

HIGHLIGHTS
• Roman ruins, especially those at Nîmes and the Pont du Gard

• Unspoiled medieval villages like Séguret

• Beautiful wine country, centered around Châteauneuf-du-Pape

• Undiscovered gems like the village of Uzès

INTRO
Northern Provence is home to impressive Roman structures like the **Pont du Gard**, the ruins found in the fortified medieval village of **Vaison-la-Romaine**, the massive theatre of **Orange**, and some of the world's best-preserved Roman sights of **Nîmes**, "the Rome of France." After you've viewed the extraordinary Roman sights, you can slow down in the quaint medieval villages of **Séguret** and **Le Barroux** or head to undiscovered **Uzès**. Top it all off by drinking the delicious wines of the vineyards of **Châteauneuf-du-Pape!**

Note: Many attractions and offices in Provence close at noon and re-open an hour or two later.

COORDINATES
Northern Provence's largest city, **Nîmes**, has a population of 140,000. The towns are within 25 miles (40km) of Avignon and about 400 miles (644km) south of Paris.

NORTHERN PROVENCE
Vaison-la-Romaine
The fortified medieval village of **Vaison-la-Romaine** seems to hang precariously over the road as you approach. It's 20 miles (32 km) northeast of Avignon/17 miles (27 km) northeast of Orange. Vaison-la-Romaine can be reached from Avignon by bus (90 minutes) and Orange by bus (45 minutes).

The village is divided into two by the Ouvèze River. The Roman bridge connects **Ville-Basse** (the Roman and present-day town) and **Ville-Haute** (the medieval town). A lively market fills **la place François-Cevert** every Tuesday morning and early afternoon.

Head to the **Roman Ruins** in the Ville-Basse. The ruins are split by a modern road (avenue Général-de-Gaulle). The **Quartier de Puyim** has remains of a 6,000-seat theatre, temples, courthouse (praeto-

rium), and foundations of homes including the **Maison des Messii.** The **Musée Théo-Desplans,** an archeology museum, is here. Across the street is the **Quartier de la Villasse** with the remains of a Roman village, including its baths (and marble toilets). *Info: In Ville Basse (avenue Général-de-Gaulle). Closed Jan 5 to Feb 8. Admission: €8 (includes admission to the cloister at Cathédral Notre-Dame-de-Nazareth, below).*

Also worth a look is the **Cathédral Notre-Dame-de-Nazareth.** One of the finest examples of Provençal Romanesque architecture, this cathedral is known for its sculpted cloister. *Info: avenue Jules Ferry. Closed Jan 5 to Feb 8. Admission: €8 (includes admission to the Roman ruins, above).*

Now it's time to head to the **Haute Ville** (Upper Town).

From the Roman ruins on avenue Général-de-Gaulle toward the river, you'll cross the 2,000-year-old **Pont Romain** (Roman bridge). In the 1990s, a flood destroyed a nearby modern bridge, but left the Roman bridge intact! Explore the fortified medieval village high above the river valley. You'll pass 13th- and 14th-century homes on your way through a twisted maze of steep cobblestone streets. At the highest point are the ruins of a castle built in 1160 by the Count of Toulouse.

While in the Upper Town, you're going to get quite hungry climbing the steep streets. A good place to relax, eat and drink is at **Les Terrasses du Beffroi** on the garden terrace at the Beffroi Hotel. *Info: rue de l'Évêché (in the Upper Town). Tel. 04/90.36.04.71. Closed Tue.*

VAISON-LA-ROMAINE SLEEPS & EATS
Hôtel Beffroi €-€€
Located in a beautiful 16th-century mansion in the Upper Town, this 22-room, family-owned hotel offers panoramic views of the surrounding area. There's a garden terrace, an outdoor pool, and parking both at the hotel (a rarity in the Upper Town) and at the foot of the Upper Town. *Info: rue de l'Évêché (in the Upper Town). www.le-beffroi. com. Tel. 04/90.36.04.71. V, MC, DC, AE. TV, telephone, hairdryer. minibar. Restaurant €€.*

SÉGURET & LE BARROUX

We'll visit two medieval villages: Séguret and Le Barroux.

The quaint medieval village of **Séguret** clings to the foothills of the **Dentelles de Montmirail**, a series of limestone rocks stretching skyward. It's five miles (nine km) southwest of Vaison-la-Romaine. You can climb its car-free and steep cobblestone streets lined with vine-covered stone homes. There are three medieval gateways, the 12th-century church **Eglise St-Denis**, a 15th-century fountain, and castle ruins. A truly lovely town. Take in the sweeping views of the vineyards on the plain below and don't leave this area without stopping at one (or a few) of them.

We recommend you unwind at **Le Mesclun**, a village restaurant serving Provençal dishes at reasonable prices. Great views of the surrounding vineyards from the outdoor terrace. *Info: rue des Poternes. Tel. 04/90 16 93.43. Closed Wed. Moderate.*

If you thought Séguret was unspoiled, wait until you see **Le Barroux**! It's ten miles (16 km) south of Vaison-la-Romaine/21 miles (34 km) northeast of Avignon. A maze of narrow streets with ancient fountains makes this unspoiled hill town worth a visit. You can tour the restored vaulted rooms of the imposing fortified *château* and Renaissance chapel. The castle is a frequent site for contemporary-art exhibits. *Info: Tel. 04/90.62.35.21. Open daily Jun-Oct. Weekends only Apr-May. Admission: €5.*

LE BARROUX SLEEPS & EATS

Les Géraniums €
This family-owned, 22-room hotel in an unspoiled hill town also has a great restaurant. Relax on the beautiful flowered terrace where meals are served. Try the *plateau de fromages de France*, a platter of de-

licious French cheeses. *Info: place de la Croix. www.hotel-lesgeraniums. Tel. 04/90.62.41.08. Closed in winter. V, MC. Restaurant (€-€€), telephone.*

ORANGE

Next up: the magnificent Roman structures of **Orange**. It's 19 miles (31 km) north of Avignon/6 miles (10 km) north of Châteauneuf-du-Pape. Orange can be reached from Avignon by bus (45 minutes) and by train (15 minutes).

Orange's name dates back to when it was governed by the Dutch House of Orange. It became a thriving Roman city filled with public baths, temples, and monuments. In the 13th century, many of the Roman buildings were demolished and the stone used to build a defensive wall. Today most visitors come to this town overlooking the Rhône Valley to see two magnificent Roman structures that survived.

The massive **Théâtre Antique** (Roman theatre) was built in the time of Caesar Augustus, and his statue on the center stage still survives. This is the best-preserved Roman theatre in the world.

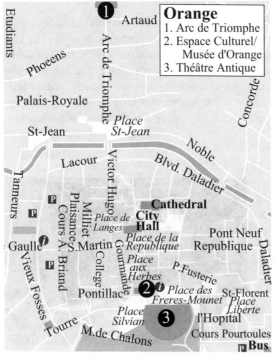

Its acoustic wall remains, and if you climb the stairs to the top of the semi-circle of theatre seats you can still hear conversations of those on the stage: a testament to the acoustical-engineering skills of its classical designers. Plays and musical events are still held here, and there's an opera and classical music fair, called Les Chorégies d'Orange, every July. An archeological dig of an ancient gymnasium is located adjacent to the theatre.

Also on the same square is the **Espace Culturel/Musée d'Orange.** This small museum displays Roman antiquities and has a gift shop. It's across the street from the Théâtre Antique. *Info: place des Frères-Mounet. www.theatre-antique.com. Tel. 04/90.51.17.60. Open Jan, Feb, Nov, and Dec 9:30am-4:30pm; Mar and Oct 9:30am-5:30pm; Apr, May and Sep 9am-6pm; Jun-Aug 9am-7pm. Admission: €9.50 (includes audio guide and entry to the Théâtre Antique, see above).*

If you're really into Roman structures, check out the **Arc de Triomphe** north of the city center at the traffic circle on avenue Arc de Triomphe (in the direction of Gap). This incredibly well-preserved 60-foot-tall Roman arch was built between 49 and 20 B.C., and is decorated with battle scenes.

There's a morning **food and flea market** on cours A.-Briand.

ORANGE SLEEPS & EATS
Hôtel Arène €-€€
Four town houses have been combined to create this unique 35-room hotel in the historic Old Town. Traditional furnishings, a helpful staff and a quiet location on a pedestrian street all make this a good option while in Orange. Some rooms have been recently renovated. *Info: Place de Langes. www.hotel-arene.fr. Tel. 04/90.11.40.40. V, MC, DC, AE. TV, telephone, minibar, hairdryer, safe, pool.*

Hôtel Le Glacier €-€€
This family-run hotel has a great location just a few blocks from the Roman Theater. Rooms vary in size, but all are clean and nicely decorated. There's also secure parking. Good choice if you want to walk to all the sights. Friendly welcome. *Info: 46 Cours Aristide Briand. www.le-glacier.com. Tel. 04/90.34.02.01. V, MC. AC, TV, WiFi.*

La Grotte d'Auguste €€
This unique restaurant, located inside the Théâtre Antique, serves Provençal fare in stone rooms and on the terrace with views of the Roman theatre (photo at right). *Info: Théâtre Antique. Tel. 06/76.04.43.83. Open daily.*

Le Bec Fin €€
White tablecloths, stone walls, and a comfortable atmosphere await you at this small restaurant near the Théâtre Antique. Try the three-course menu (€25) and try the delicious *terrine de lapin* (rabbit terrine) and the *magret de canard* (duck breast) served in a citrus sauce. *Info: 14 rue Segond Weber (at rue Petite Fusterie). www.restaurant-le-bec-fin.fr. Tel. 04/90.66.63.84. Closed Sun.*

WINE TASTING
You're in the heart of wine country. Look for signs saying **Cave Coopérative** at vineyards. If they say *dégustation*, this means free wine tastings are offered. Although there's no obligation to buy, you should get at least one bottle (especially if you've spent some time at the winery).

CHÂTEAUNEUF-DU-PAPE
Get ready to drink some wine in **Châteauneuf-du-Pape**. It's 6 miles (10 km) south of Orange/14 miles (23 km) west of Carpentras/11 miles (18 km) north of Avignon.

This town's history is linked to the popes of Avignon. The château towering over the town was built by the popes in the 14th century as a summer residence, and was badly damaged by bombing during World War II. Vineyards, said to have been planted by the popes, surround the lovingly restored town whose names means "new castle of the pope." Today, the wines from this area are known the world over. In 1954 the village council passed an ordinance prohibiting the landing of flying saucers (they called them "flying cigars") in their vineyards. (This ordinance has worked well in discouraging such landings).

The **Fête de la Véraison** (wine festival) is held for three days in early August. Locals dress in medieval costumes, and area wineries set up stalls. For about €5, you purchase a souvenir glass and sample all the wine you want. If you start seeing wine coming out of the attractive fountain in the place du Portail, you're not that drunk; it really does spurt wine during the festival.

After exploring the town, head to route D17, and stop at the **Musée du Vin/Caves Brotte**. Located in the cellar (cave) of a family winery, this museum celebrates the area's wine making tradition. And yes, there are wine tastings. *Info: avenue le Bienheureux Pierre du Luxembourg (route D17). Tel. 04/90.83.70.07. Open daily. Admission: Free.*

There are over 20 area wineries where you can taste the wines of Châteauneuf-du-Pape. **Clos des Papes** is conveniently located on the route to Avignon. *Info: 13 avenue le Bienheureux Pierre du Luxembourg (route D17). Tel. 04/90.83.70.13. Open daily.*

CHÂTEAUNEUF-DU-PAPE EATS
Le Pistou €-€€
This restaurant takes its name from *pistou* (a sauce made of garlic, basil, nuts and olive oil), the Provençal version of Italian pesto. Several dishes feature *pistou*, such as the delicious *soup au pistou*. Local dishes at very reasonable prices. *Info: 15 ruc Joseph-Ducos (near the Hôtel de Ville (City Hall)). Tel. 04/90.83.71.75. Closed Sun (dinner) and Mon.*

La Maisouneta €€
This friendly and comfortable restaurant serves Provençal specialties. It's conveniently located in the center of this attractive town. The house specialty is *magret de canard* (duck breast). Try the grilled version with honey and lavender. Good selection of *pâtes fraiches* (fresh pasta dishes). A good selection of local wines is available and there are occasional wine tastings. *Info: 7 rue Joseph Ducos (at rue Frédéric Mistral). www.la-maisouneta.fr. Tel. 04/90.32.55.03. Closed Tue (dinner), Wed, and part of Jan.*

Château des Fines Roches €€-€€€
This 11-room hotel is quite unique. It's located in a former *château*. The 19th-century building has been renovated and has been a hotel since the 1970s. It's conveniently located outside of Châteaunuef-du-Pape

and only six miles from Avignon. Fabulous swimming pool and beautiful views of the surrounding vineyards. *Info: Route de Sorgues. www.chateaufinesroches.com. Tel. 04/90.83.70.23.*

The gourmet restaurant here, **La Table des Fines Roches** (€€€) serves innovative French and Provençal cuisine. The restaurant's terrace is a lovely place to dine. The *cave* (wine cellar) here is known for its great selection of wines from Châteaunuef-du-Pape. *Info: This is a great choice to dine at lunch. The menu (a starter and main dish or main dish and dessert) costs €26. Closed Mon.*

PONT DU GARD

Today we'll view Roman ingenuity at the **Pont du Gard** (see photo on page 92). It's 23 miles (37 km) southwest of Orange/13 miles (22 km) southwest of Avignon. Pont du Gard can be reached from Avignon by bus (50 minutes).

How did they do it? Two thousand years ago, the Romans built a system to carry water 30 miles from a spring near Uzès to Nîmes. The Pont du Gard is a huge three-tiered, arched aqueduct spanning the **Gardon River.** It's the second tallest Roman structure in the world. Only the Coliseum in Rome is taller.

The aqueduct once carried 44 million gallons each day. The 80-foot main arch is the largest ever built by the Romans. When we first visited the aqueduct, you were able to walk on the very top (a scary and dangerous experience).

WINE WORDS

wine, *vin*
wine list, *carte des vins*
red wine, *vin rouge*
rosé wine, *vin rosé*
white wine, *vin blanc*
bottle, *bouteille*
half-bottle, *demi-bouteille*
glass, *verre*
full-bodied, *robuste*

Today, the aqueduct is off-limits. Visitors flock here and marvel at the sheer size of this tribute to Roman ingenuity. A **museum** at the visitor center highlights the history of the aqueduct, and there's an informative film that plays every half hour. Ludo is an interactive kids' zone (in English). There's a café for light meals and a restaurant offering regional specialties. You can swim in the river below, dive off part of the aqueduct, or rent a canoe (which is a great way to experience the aqueduct). *Info: www.pontdugard.fr. Tel. 04/66.37.50.99. Open daily 9am-5pm (Mar to May and Oct to 6pm, Jun and Sep to 7pm, Jul and Aug to 8pm). A ticket for parking and the museums can be purchased for €18.*

UZÈS

Don't bypass **Uzès** on the border of Provence in the Languedoc region. It's 15 miles (25 km) north of Nîmes/24 miles (39 km) west of Avignon. Uzès can be reached from Avignon by bus (80 minutes).

Begin your visit to this lovely town at the imposing **Cathédrale St-**

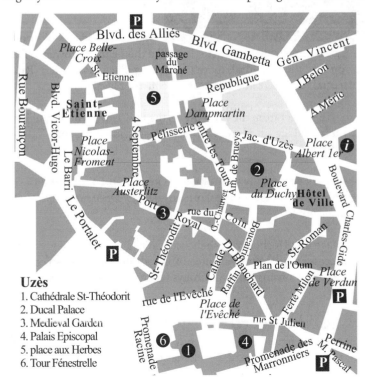

Uzès
1. Cathédrale St-Théodorit
2. Ducal Palace
3. Medieval Garden
4. Palais Episcopal
5. place aux Herbes
6. Tour Fénestrelle

Théodorit (you can't miss it, and there's a large car park next to it). The cathedral, built on the site of a Roman temple, dates back to 1652. Those are the remains of St-Firmin in the glass coffin on the left side of the cathedral.

Organ concerts are held in the Cathédrale St-Théodorit, especially the last two weeks of July, during the musical festival Nuits Musicales d'Uzès. The concerts are played on its 2,700-pipe organ which dates back to the 17th century.

When outside, look up at the Tour Fénestrelle. Doesn't it look like the Leaning Tower of Pisa? As you face the cathedral, there's a former palace to your left (Palais Episcopal) that now houses the city's courts of law.

Across the street from the cathedral is the Old Town where you'll find the ducal palace on place du Duché. Descendents of the House of Uzès still live here.

Take a walk around the beautiful and car-free Old Town, and to visit the medieval garden on rue Port Royal. *Info: Open daily Apr to Oct, admission: €4.50.*

The place aux Herbes with sheltered walkways and medieval homes is a relaxing place to take a coffee break, although it's not so calm on Wednesday mornings and Saturdays when it hosts a lively market.

UZÈS SLEEPS & EATS
Hôtel Entraigues €€-€€€
This 36-room hotel is housed in converted 17th- and 18th- century private homes near the cathedral. It was completely renovated in 2015.

It has a lovely swimming pool and a good restaurant, serving food on the terrace. *Info: 8 rue de la Calade (at place de l'Évêché). www.hotel-en-traigues.com. Tel. 04/66.72.05.25. V, MC, AE. Restaurant, bar, outdoor pool, AC, TV, telephone, minibar, hairdryer, safe.*

La Table d'Uzès €€-€€€ This award-winning restaurant will not disappoint. Dine indoors or outdoors in the attractive courtyard. The €30 lunch menu includes a glass of wine. Try the flavorful *filet mignon de porc*! The restaurant has a large selection of wines from the Languedoc region. Located in the lovely La Maison d'Uzès Hotel (€€€). *Info: 18 rue Docteur Blanchard. Tel. 04/66.20.07.00. www.lamaison-duzes.fr. Open daily.*

NÎMES
Officially part of the Languedoc region, **Nîmes** is a popular destination for visitors to Provence. It's 26 miles (43 km) southwest of Avignon/19 miles (31 km) northwest of Arles. Nîmes can be reached from Avignon by bus (30 minutes) and by train (30 minutes).

Some of the world's best-preserved Roman sights are here, giving it the nickname "the Rome of France." The town is dotted with Roman ruins. It's frenetic and not at all like the calm small villages of Provence. Did you know that denim (the material that all those jeans are made of) was created here in the Middle Ages? The Old Town is easily explored on foot, and is home to the major sights.

Head to the tourist office at 6 rue Auguste where you can pick up a free map. It's near the first site that we'll visit (you can't miss it).

The steel-and-glass **Carré d'Art** is home to a contemporary art museum featuring works created after 1960. You can stop for refreshments at the rooftop café here. It has a great view of the Roman temple and

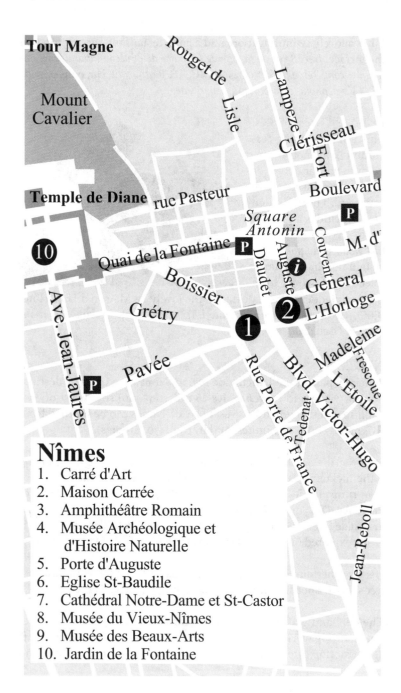

Nîmes
1. Carré d'Art
2. Maison Carrée
3. Amphithéâtre Romain
4. Musée Archéologique et
   d'Histoire Naturelle
5. Porte d'Auguste
6. Eglise St-Baudile
7. Cathédral Notre-Dame et St-Castor
8. Musée du Vieux-Nîmes
9. Musée des Beaux-Arts
10. Jardin de la Fontaine

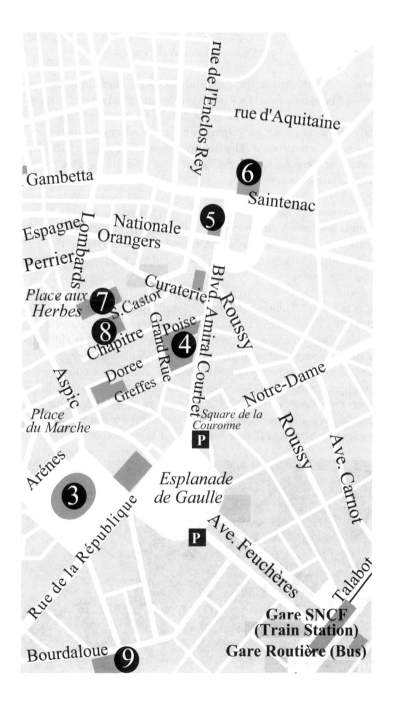

other landmarks. *Info: place de la Maison Carrée. Tel. 04/66.76.35.70. Open Tue-Sun 10am-6pm. Closed Mon. Admission: €5.*

Head across the street. Built around 5 B.C., the incredibly well-preserved **Maison Carrée** is a Roman temple modeled after the Temple of Apollo in Rome. It was the model for the Eglise de la Madeleine in Paris, the state capitol of Virginia, and many other buildings featuring Corinthian columns. The interior houses changing exhibits. *Info: place de la Comédie (boulevard Victor-Hugo). Tel. 04/66.21.82.56. Open daily. Admission: €6.*

As you leave the Roman temple, the street between it and the art museum is boulevard Victor Hugo. Head down the boulevard in the opposite direction of the tourist-information shop. You'll pass the place de la Madeleine (to your right on boulevard Victor Hugo). Soon you'll see a large arena.

Look familiar? The well-preserved **Amphithéâtre Romain** (Roman arena) is a miniature of the Colosseum in Rome. It held over 20,000 people who watched gladiators fight. Today, it's used for performances and an occasional bullfight. In the 13th century, the arena was inhabited by nearly 700 people who created a miniature village inside. Napoleon changed all that when he designated it a historic monument. *Info: place de Arènes. Tel. 04/66.21.82.56. Open daily 9:30am-5pm (Jan, Feb, Nov, and Dec), 9am-6pm (Mar and Oct), 9am-6:30pm (Apr, May, and Sep), 9am-7pm (Jun), 9am-8pm (Jul and Aug). Admission: €9.50.*

Across the street from the arena is the **Musée des Cultures Taurines**, a bull-fighting museum, at 6 rue Alexandre-Ducros. *Info: Tel. 04/66.36.83.77. Open Tue-Sun 10am-6pm. Closed Mon. Admission: €5.*

Other sights of interest here include the following three on boulevard de l'Amiral-Courbet:

The **Musée Archéologique et d'Histoire Naturelle**, a museum of archaeology and natural history, is filled with statues, friezes, pottery, and coins. *Info: 13 bis boulevard de l'Amiral-Courbet. Tel. 04/66.76.74.80. Open Tue-Sun 10am-6pm. Closed Mon. Admission: Free.*

TOP ROMAN SIGHTS

• The **Pont du Gard**, a huge three-tiered, arched aqueduct spanning the Gardon River (13 miles southwest of Avignon)
• **La Trophée des Alpes**, towering over the village of La Turbie in the hills above Monaco
• The **theater and arena** in Arles
• The ruins and 2,000-year-old **Pont Romain** (bridge) in Vaison-la-Romaine
• The **Théâtre Antique and Arc de Triomphe** in Orange
• The **Glanum/Les Antiques** ruins (a Gallo-Roman village) in St-Rémy
• The **theatre, arena and aqueduct** in Fréjus
• The **Roman gate and tower** in Nîmes

The **Porte d'Auguste** is a gate built during the reign of Augustus. Across the street is the church Eglise St-Baudile, named after the martyr and patron saint of the city.

In the Old Town are two sights next to each other that are worth a visit.

The **Cathédral Notre-Dame et St-Castor** has a beautifully preserved Romanesque frieze featuring Adam, Eve, Abel, and Noah. Construction began on this cathedral in 1096. The inside features a 4th-century sarcophagus. *Info: place aux Herbes. Open daily. Admission: Free.*

Off of place aux Herbes (near the cathedral) is the **Musée du Vieux-Nîmes** (Museum of Old Nîmes) showcasing life in Nîmes in the Middles Ages, including a 14th-century jacket made of the famous

PÉTANQUE

What game are all those men playing in squares throughout Provence? **Pétanque**, also called **boules**, is played in every Provençal village. A *boule* is a metal ball the size of a baseball. The player who gets his *boule* closest to the target ball (*le cochonnet*) wins. Okay, this is a very simplified version of the game, but you get the picture: French lawn bowling, but it's played on sand!

denim de Nîmes, the fabric that Levi-Stauss used for blue jeans. *Info: Place aux Herbes. Tel. 04/66.76.73.70. Open Tue-Sun 10am-6pm. Closed Mon. Admission: Free.*

The **Musée des Beaux-Arts** is the city's fine-arts museum. The museum is itself a work of art and is located in the former residence of a Ukrainian princess. You'll find not only French paintings and sculpture, but also a large collection of Flemish and Italian paintings, including Ruben's *Portrait of a Monk*. A well-preserved Gallo-Roman mosaic is also here as is Rodin's imposing sculpture The Kiss. *Info: rue de la Cité-Foulc. Tel. 04/66.67.38.21. Open Tue-Sun 10am-6pm. Closed Mon. Admission: Free.*

One of the most beautiful gardens in all of France is the **Jardin de la Fontaine**. Designed in the 18th century, the chestnut trees shade statues, urns, and the remains of a Roman shrine. At the end of the garden are the ruins of the 1st-century Temple de Diane. Also here is the Tour Magne (a tower on Mont Cavalier and the city's oldest monument). *Info: End of quai de la Fontaine. Open daily. Admission: Free.*

NÎMES SLEEPS & EATS
Imperator Concorde €€-€€€
This recently renovated 60-room hotel is located near one of the most beautiful gardens in all of France, the Jardin de la Fontaine. Rooms are decorated with traditional regional furnishings, and the bathrooms are quite modern. The lovely restaurant, **L'Enclos de la Fontaine,** serves local special-

ties, and the Hemingway bar opens onto the peaceful garden. *Info: Quai de la Fontaine. www.hotel-imperator.com. Tel. 04/66.21.90.30. V, MC, DC, AE. Restaurant, bar, AC, TV, telephone, minibar, hairdryer, safe.*

Hôtel l'Amphithéâtre €

This 15-room hotel is the budget choice in Nîmes. Located in an 18th-century, formerly private home, it's crammed with antiques. You may feel a little cramped in the small rooms (with small bathrooms), but the price and location are right. *Info: 4 rue des Arènes. Tel. 04/66.67.28.51. www.hoteldelaamphitheatre.com. V, MC. TV, AC. Closed most of Jan.*

Hôtel des Tuileries €

Located near the Arènes and the train station, this hotel features 10 guest rooms and one suite. Comfortable rooms have small balconies. The owners are from the U.K. and extremely helpful and friendly. Good value. *Info: 2 rue Roussy. www.hoteldestuileries.com. Tel. 04/66.21.31.15. V, MC. TV, AC, hairdryer, refrigerator, safe, WiFi, parking.*

Skab €€€

This modern and elegant restaurant is located near the arena. Innovative Provençal cuisine and friendly service. Try the *pintade* (guinea hen) with *fleurs de courgettes* (zucchini flowers stuffed with cheese). Extensive wine list. *Info: 7 rue de la République. Tel. 04/66.21.94.30. www. restaurant-skab.fr. Closed Sun and Mon.*

Le Vintage Café €€

This popular wine bar in the Old Town serves local food at reasonable prices. Try the *gazpacho* or *magret de canard* (duck breast) served in an apricot sauce. *Info: 7 rue de Bernis. Tel. 04/66.21.04.45. Closed Sat (lunch), Sun and Mon.*

Le Ciel de Nîmes €€

This restaurant and café is located on the terrace atop the contemporary art museum Carré d'Art. Relax while you take in a great view of the city's sights. *Info: place de la Maison Carrée. www.lecieldenimes.fr. Tel. 04/66.36.71.70. Open 10am-6pm. Closed Mon. Open some evenings for dinner in summer.*

There are lively cafés on boulevard Victor-Hugo and the area around the place de la Maison Carrée. You'll find plenty of cafés at the lively **place de l'Horloge** (Clock Square).

NÎMES NIGHTLIFE & ENTERTAINMENT
Northern Provence is not known for its nightlife. Your best bet here is Nîmes.

La Comédie is a popular dance club. *Info: 28 rue Jean-Reboul. Tel. 04/66.76.13.66*

There are several **gay and gay-friendly** establishments in Nîmes:
- **Lulu,** *10 impasse de la Curaterie, Tel. 04/66.36.28.20 (nightclub)*
- **Le Little,** *1 rue Thoumayne, Tel. 06/52.44.77.27 (bar)*
- **Fahrenheit 212,** *1606 ave. Marechal Juin, Tel. 04/66.38.24.76 (sauna)*
- **Nîmes Sauna Club,** *7 rue F. Pelloutier, Tel. 04/66.67.65.18 (sauna).*

7. Avignon

HIGHLIGHTS

• The place de l'Horloge, the heart of the city

• The colossal Papal Palace where two popes ruled,
and the Cathedral

• La Fondation Angladon-Dubrujeaud, with art by Picasso,
van Gogh, Degas, Cézanne...

• The famous bridge with its four arches

• Lovely bistros, cafes, restaurants and hotels

INTRO

In 1309, when **Pope Clément V** arrived after fleeing the corruption of Rome, the town became the capital of Christendom for 68 years. Although the last pope left in 1377, you're reminded of the **papal legacy** everywhere in modern-day **Avignon**. Its large student population makes it a vibrant city, unlike most of the small villages of Provence.

The students, upscale boutiques and crowded cafés all make Avignon the most cosmopolitan city in Provence.

COORDINATES

Avignon (population 90,000) is in the south of France. It's 60 miles (100km) inland from the Mediterranean port city of Marseille, 51 miles (82km) northeast of Aix-en-Provence, and 425 miles (685 km) south of Paris. Start your visit to Avignon by entering through the **Porte de la République**, one of the entries through the massive walls built by the Church. It's near the train station and parking lots. The tourist office is at 41 cours Jean-Jaurés.

Avignon has a **TGV** (fast-speed train) station on the edge of town. The TGV station is connected to the Avignon Centre-Ville Station (in the central city) by TER, a local train. For more information on train travel to Avignon, see the *Practical Matters* chapter.

You can reach other destinations in Provence from Avignon by bus or train:
• L'Isle-sur-la-Sorgue: 45 minutes by bus/30 minutes by train
• Orange: 45 minutes by bus/15 minutes by train
• Nîmes: 30 minutes by bus/30 minutes by train
• Arles: 60 minutes by bus/20 minutes by train
• St-Rémy-de-Provence: 45 minutes by bus
• Pont du Gard: 50 minutes by bus
• Le Baux: 65 minutes by bus
• Uzès: 80 minutes by bus
• Vaison-la-Romaine: 90 minutes by bus.

SIGHTS

Musée Lapidaire

This museum is located in a Jesuit chapel, and is filled with a collection of sculpture and stonework from the 1st and 2nd centuries. *Info: 27 rue de la République (at the corner of rue Frédéric Mistral). www. musee-lapidaire.org. Tel. 04/90.85.75.38. Open Wed-Mon 10am-1pm and 2pm-6pm. Closed Tue. Admission: €2.*

La Fondation Angladon-Dubrujeaud

This museum is filled with the works of Picasso, van Gogh, Degas, Modigliani and Cézanne, to name a few. There's also a collection of furniture and art objects. *Info: 5 rue Laboureur (at the end of rue Frédéric Mistral). www.angladon.com. Tel. 04/90.82.29.03. Open Wed-Sun 1pm-6pm. Closed Mon and Tue. (Open Tue in summer.) Admission: €6.50.*

place de l'Horloge
This is the heart of the city, filled with bistros, cafés, and restaurants. It gets its name from the Gothic **Tour du Jacquemart** (clock tower). Great people-watching! On the square are the **Hôtel de Ville** (City Hall) and the 19th-century **Opéra House**. This square is a great place to take a break. Why don't you try a *pastis* (anise-flavored *aperitif*)? A Provençal word meaning mixture, it's a summer drink. Common brands are Pastis 51, Pernod, Ricard, Granier, Prado and Henri Bardouin. *Info: On rue de la République. Just off the place de l'Horloge is the place du Palais (rue Phillipe connects the two places).*

Palais des Papes (Papal Palace)
In 1309, French Pope Clément V was elected and moved to Avignon from Rome. For 68 years, popes ruled from here. In 1378, there were competing popes (one in Rome and one here). This schism continued until 1417. The popes in Avignon during this schism are referred to as the "antipopes." Benedict XII, the third pope to rule from Avignon, ordered the construction of this colossal palace that dominates Avignon. Today, you can tour the large palace. Be warned, it's mostly empty. The Great Court links the **Palais Vieux** (Old Palace) with the more decorated **Palais Nouveau** (New Palace).

Some highlights are:
- **Chapelle St-Jean:** with its frescoes of the life of John the Baptist
- **Chapelle St-Martial:** with its frescoes of the miracles of St. Martial
- **Grand Tinel** (Banquet Hall): with vaulted roof and 18th-century tapestries

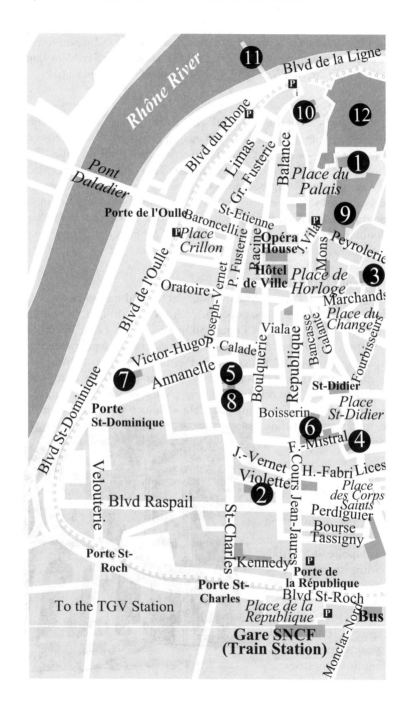

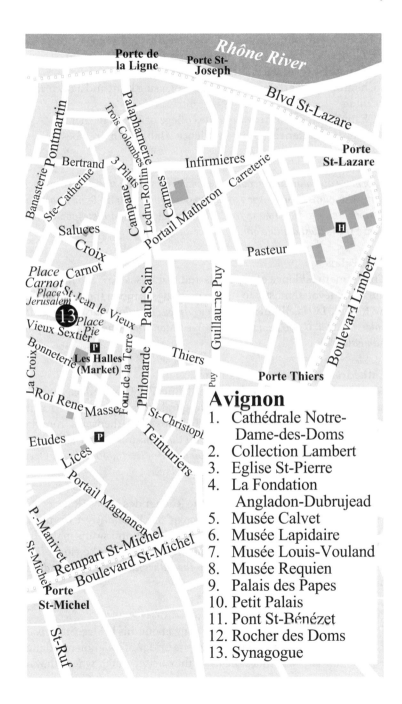

Porte de
la Ligne

Porte St-
Joseph

Rhône River

Blvd St-Lazare

Porte
St-Lazare

Banasterie Pontmartin

Palapharmerie

Trois Colombes

Bertrand

Ste-Catherine

3 Pilats

Campane

Ledru-Rollin

Carmes

Infirmieres

Portail Matheron

Carreterie

Saluces

Croix

Pasteur

H

Place Carnot

Carnot

Place
Jerusalem

St-Jean le Vieux

Place
Pie

Paul-Sain

Guillaume Puy

Boulevard Limbert

13

Vieux Sextier

Bonneterie

La Croix

Les Halles
(Market)

Four de la Terre

Philonarde

Thiers

Puy

Porte Thiers

Roi Rene

Masse

St-Christophe

Etudes

P

Teinturiers

Lices

Portail Magnanen

P.-Manivet

St-Michel

Rempart St-Michel

Boulevard St-Michel

Porte
St-Michel

St-Ruf

Avignon

1. Cathédrale Notre-
   Dame-des-Doms
2. Collection Lambert
3. Eglise St-Pierre
4. La Fondation
   Angladon-Dubrujead
5. Musée Calvet
6. Musée Lapidaire
7. Musée Louis-Vouland
8. Musée Requien
9. Palais des Papes
10. Petit Palais
11. Pont St-Bénézet
12. Rocher des Doms
13. Synagogue

- **Pope's Chamber:** the pontiff slept in this bedroom, whose blue walls are decorated with a vine-leaf motif
- **Consistoire** (Council Hall): with 14th-century frescoes
- **Chambre du Cerf:** featuring murals of a stag hunt and a decorated ceiling
- **Chapelle Clémentine:** where the college of cardinals met
- **Grande Audience** (Great Audience Hall): with frescoes of the prophets

Info: place du Palais. www.palais-des-papes.com. Tel. 04/90.27.50.00. Open daily Mar 9am-6:30pm, Apr 1 to Jun 30 9am-7pm, Jul 9am-8pm, Aug 9am-8:30pm, Sep 1 to Nov 1 9am-7pm, Nov 2 to Feb 29 9:30am-5:45pm. Admission: €11 (including audio guide); under 8 free.

Petit Palais
The former residence of cardinals and bishops is now the home of a museum devoted mostly to Italian paintings. Among them are works by Bellini, Botticelli and Carpaccio. *Info: place du Palais. www.petit-palais.org. Tel. 04/90.86.44.58. Open Wed-Mon 10am-1pm and 2pm-6pm. Admission: €6.*

Cathédrale Notre-Dame-des-Doms
Some of the popes who ruled from the nearby Papal Palace are buried here in the Gothic tomb. The cathedral dates back to the 12th century. The gold statue of the Virgin that tops the cathedral is from the 19th century. *Info: place du Palais (with the cathedral to your back) head through the gates). www.cathedrale-avignon.fr. Tel. 04/90.86.81.01. Open daily 9am-noon and 2pm-6pm. Admission: Free.*

On the hill next to the cathedral is the **Rocher des Doms** (Rock of the Domes). You can enjoy the views across the Rhône River from this rocky bluff and garden. Huge pine trees, statues and swans make this a great place to relax. There's a small vineyard down the slope. *Info: Montée du Moulin (on the hill next to the cathedral). Open daily. Admission: Free.*

Pont St-Bénézet (St. Bénézet Bridge)
There's a famous French children's song about this bridge: *Sur le pont d'Avignon on y danse, on y danse...* ("On the bridge of Avignon one dances, one dances..."). If that's the case, they better watch where they're

stepping, as this arched bridge stretches across only part of the river. Legend has it that a shepherd named Bénézet was told by an angel to begin building the bridge in 1177. Only four arches of the original 22 remain, the rest having been destroyed by floods and war. There's a chapel on the bridge, and a small museum of the history of the bridge. *Info: rue Ferruce. Open daily 9:30am-5:45pm (Jul-Sep until 8pm). Admission: €5 (audio guide included).*

Synagogue
Avignon's synagogue dates back to the 1200s. There's a memorial to Jews deported from here to the concentration camp at Auschwitz. *Info: rue Bernheim-Lyon (off of rue du Vieux Sextier). Closed some Sat and Sun. Admission: Free.*

Eglise St-Pierre
You can admire the Gothic façade of a 12th-century church. The 16th-century carved doors depict the Annunciation, when the angel Gabrielle informed Mary that she would conceive a son. *Info: place St-Pierre/rue des Ciseaux d'Or. Open daily. Admission: Free.*

Musée Requien
This is one of the largest natural-history libraries in France. Most come to visit its herbarium which contains more than 200,000 specimens gathered by botanists from around the world. There's also an exhibit featuring the botany of Provence. *Info: 67 rue Joseph-Vernet. www.museum-requien.org. Tel. 04/90.82.43.51. Open 10am-1pm and 2pm-6pm. Closed Sun and Mon. Admission: Free.*

Musée Calvet
Located in a beautiful 18th-century mansion, this museum (with a

lovely garden) maintains a collection of antiquities (some of which are housed at the Musée Lapidaire above), and works by Manet, Brueghel, Corot and David. *Info: 65 rue Joseph-Vernet. Tel. 04/90.86.33.84. www.musee-calvert.org. Open Wed-Mon 10am-1pm and 2pm-6pm. Closed Tue. Admission: €6.*

Musée Louis-Vouland

Located in a 19th-century mansion, this museum is filled with 17th- and 18th-century antiques, tapestries and art objects. *Info: 17 rue Victor-Hugo. Tel. 04/90.86.03.79. Open Tue-Sun noon-6pm (2pm 6pm in winter). Closed Mon and Feb. Admission: €6.*

Collection Lambert

The exterior of this 18th-century mansion doesn't look anything like the contemporary art housed inside. The museum houses the collection of Yvon Lambert. This collection includes more than 1200 work of art dating from the 1960s to present. Interesting special exhibits. *Info: 5 rue Violette. www.collectionlambert.com. Tel. 04/90.16.56.20. Open Tue-Sun 11am-6pm. Open daily Jul and Aug 11am-7pm. Admission: €10.*

Villeneuve-lès-Avignon

If you want to get away from Avignon but don't want to drive, cross the Rhône River to Villeneuve-lès-Avignon. Villeneuve means "new city" and refers to the area across the **Pont Daladier** from Avignon

(bus 11 runs between the two cities). In the 1300s, cardinals built private estates here. The **Fort St-André** dominates the hilltop (*see photo on previous page*). The 13th-century **Tour Philippe le Bel** affords great views of Avignon and the Rhône Valley. *Info: rue Montée-de-la-Tour. Tel. 04/32.70.08.57. Open May to Oct 10am-12:30pm and 2pm-6pm. Feb to Apr 2pm-6pm. Closed Mon and Nov-Jan. Admission: €2.50.*

Musée Municipal Pierre-de-Luxembourg
The former residence of cardinals is now the home of a museum loaded with medieval sculpture and paintings. *Info: rue de la République. Tel. 04/90.27.49.66. Open May to Oct Tue-Sun 10am-12:30pm and 2pm-6pm. Feb to Apr and Nov to Dec Tue-Sun 2pm-5pm. Closed Mon and Jan. Admission: €3.60.*

Chartreuse du Val-de-Bénédiction
Built in 1352, this is France's largest monastery. It was founded by Pope Innocent VI, who is buried here. You can visit the church, three cloisters, monastic cells and splendid gardens. *Info: 60 rue de la République Tel. 04/90.15.24.24. Open daily 9:30am-6:30pm (Oct to Mar 10am-5pm). Admission: €8.*

Eglise Notre-Dame
This church dates back to the 1300s and has lovely statues and a lavish 18th-century altar. *Info: place Meissonier. Tel. 04/90.25.61.55. Open daily 10am-noon and 2pm-5pm. Admission: Free.*

BEST SLEEPS & EATS
Hôtel de la Mirande €€€
This 20-room hotel, located in a 700-year-old town house behind the Papal Palace, is luxurious, comfortable and elegant (with a renowned restaurant, too). Rooms are filled with antiques (number 20 is the most sought after). Truly an experience. *Info: 4 place de la Mirande. www.la-mirande.fr. Tel. 04/90.14.20.20. V, MC, DC, AE. Restaurant, bar, TV, AC, telephone, minibar, hairdryer, safe, WiFi.*

Hôtel d'Europe €€€ A hotel since 1799 in a building dating back to the 1580s, this award-winning 44-room hotel is known for its central location, attentive service, and excellent restaurant, **La Vielle Fontaine.** Its three suites have private terraces overlooking the Papal Palace. *Info: 14 place Crillon. www.heurope.com. Tel. 04/90.14.76.76. V, MC, DC, AE. Restaurant, bar, TV, AC, telephone, minibar, hairdryer, safe, WiFi.*

Cloître St-Louis €€

Located in a historic 16th-century building, this hotel has 80 rooms with modern furnishings, a pool, the restaurant **Le St-Louis** located under vaulted ceilings, and comfortable lounges. *Info: 20 rue du Portail Boquier. www.cloitre-saint-louis.com. Tel. 04/90.27.55.55. V, MC, AE. AC, TV, telephone, minibar, safe, hairdryer, Internet access.*

Mercure Pont d'Avignon €€

This hotel, part of a chain (with hotels in Marseille, Aix and Nice), has 87 rooms, all with small bathrooms. Its central location can't be beat as it's near the foot of the Papal Palace. *Info: rue Ferruce. www.mercure. com. Tel. 04/90.80.93.93. V, MC, DC, AE. Bar, TV, AC, telephone, minibar, hairdryer, safe, WiFi.*

Le Médiéval €

Located in an 18th-century town house, this 34-room hotel has an excellent location, only three blocks south of the Papal Palace. Decent-sized rooms with beamed ceilings have tub/shower combinations in the bathrooms. Ask for a room on the courtyard rather than the noisy street. *Info: 15 rue Petite Saunerie. www.hotelmedieval.com. Tel. 04/90.86.11.06. V, MC. TV, telephone, Internet access, hairdryer.*

La Mirande €€€

This renowned restaurant, located in a hotel in a converted 700-year-old town house behind the Papal Palace, offers elegant French dining. *Info: 4 place de la Mirande. www.la-mirande.fr. Tel. 04/90.14.20.20. Reservations required.*

Le 46 €€-€€€

This elegant restaurant is a great spot for lunch or dinner after visiting the Papal Palace. French cuisine  with a Provençal touch. **Le Bar à Vin** (Wine Bar) features wines from throughout France and Europe with an emphasis on local producers. There are usually at least 12 wines by the glass offered (along with cheese-and-meat platters). *Info: 46 rue de la Balance. www.le46avignon. com. Tel. 04/90.85.24.83. Closed Sun (except in summer).*

Hiély-Lucullus €€€

Fine French dining, such as grilled lamb and fresh fish, at a lovely centrally located restaurant. *Info: 5 rue de la République. www.hiely lucullus.com. Tel. 04/90.86.17.07. Reservations required. Closed Tue and Wed.*

La Fourchette €€-€€€

French cuisine at this cozy restaurant a block from place de l'Horloge. Try the delicious *suprême de volaille à l'estragon* (chicken breast served in a tarragon sauce). *Info: 17 rue Racine. www.la-fourchette.net. Tel. 04/90.85.20.93. Closed weekends and part of Aug.*

Ginette et Marcele €

This café is located on a picturesque square. You can dine in the shade or inside surrounded by shelves brimming with bottles of wine and canned Provençal specialties. It's known for its tasty *tartines* (open-faced sandwiches). Our favorite is the *chèvre miel* (goat cheese and honey). Delicious simple salads. *Info: 27 place des Corps Saints (off of rue des Lices). Tel. 04/90.85.58.70.*

BEST SHOPPING
Les Halles

This large covered market was built in the 1970s. Stinky fish, stinky cheese and lots of other stuff. There are over 40 stalls here. A great place to gather goods for a cheap meal or picnic. *Info: place Pie. www.*

avignon-leshalles.com. Open Tue-Fri 6am-1:30pm, Sat and Sun 6am-2pm. Closed Mon.

There is a **flower market** at place des Carmes (Saturday mornings), and a **flea market** at place des Carmes (Sunday mornings).

Pure Lavande/Le Château du Bois
For all your lavender needs! You can purchase cosmetics, beauty supplies, soaps, and gifts all featuring lavender. *Info: 61 rue Grand Fusterie. www.purelavande.com. Tel. 04/90.14.70.05. Open daily.*

Villeneuve-lès-Avignon
All sorts of antiques and *brocantes* (secondhand goods) available at an outdoor market at place du Marché on Saturday mornings.

BEST NIGHTLIFE & ENTERTAINMENT
Les Ambassadeurs
Avignon's popular dance club. Drinks from €8. *Info: 27 rue Bancasse. www.clublesambassadeurs.fr. Tel.04/90.86.31.55.*

Avignon has several **gay and gay-friendly** establishments:
• **L'Esclav:** *12 rue de Limas, Tel.04/90.85.14.91. (popular bar and disco).*
• **Cid Café:** *11 place de l'Horloge, Tel. 04/90.82.30.38 (bar)*
• **Exes:** *4 blvd. Saint Michel, Tel. 04/90.85.06.03. (sauna).*

The **Festival d'Avignon**, an annual festival of dance, theater and music is held most of July and the first week of August in Avignon (*see photo on page 111*). The squares are full of street performers, from good to absolutely awful. Can you say "mimes?" *Info: www.festival-avignon.com.*

8. Luberon

HIGHLIGHTS
- The markets and shops of L'Isle-sur-la-Sorgue

- Fontaine-de-Vaucluse, the "Niagara Falls of Provence"

- Gordes, Roussillon, Saignon and Lourmain –
  the latter a true gastronome's delight

INTRO
Just a short distance from Avignon and Aix-en-Provence by car, the towns of the **Luberon region** are our favorites. From canals and antique shops in **L'Isle-sur-la-Sorgue** to fine dining in **Lourmarin** to truly unspoiled villages like **Cucuron**, this area offers the perfect vacation. This is the heart of the market area; nearly every town has a great one, and these otherwise quiet towns come to life on market day.

L'Isle-sur-la-Sorgue is called the Venice of Provence; the majestic **Fontaine-de-Vaucluse** is sometimes referred to as the Niagara Falls of Provence. Walk around the picturesque village of **Gordes** and visit other beautiful small towns in the region, with their lavender fields, lovely markets, and wonderful hotels, restaurants and cafés.

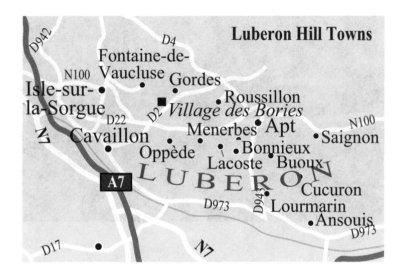

COORDINATES

The small towns of the **Luberon region** are just a short distance (20-30 miles [32-48 km]) from Avignon and Aix-en-Provence.

L'ISLE-SUR-LA-SORGUE

L'Isle-sur-la-Sorgue is 16 miles (26 km) east of Avignon/25 miles (40 km) southeast of Orange. L'Isle-sur-la-Sorgue can be reached from Avignon by bus (45 minutes) and by train (30 minutes).

The name means "Island on the Sorgue River," and is often referred to as the "Venice of Provence." We love this valley town. You'll find pedestrian bridges with flower boxes crossing graceful canals. Nine moss-covered waterwheels (that once powered the town's paper, silk and wool mills) remain along the canals.

Only Paris is said to have more antique and secondhand shops in France. There are more than 300 shops in this little town. Most are open daily. There's a huge antique fair at Easter. Try **Galerie aux Trouvailles**. This indoor antique center has 20 shops selling everything from furniture to household goods. *Info: 12 la Petit Marine. Tel. 04/90.21.14.31. Closed Tue and Wed.*

In the center of the Old Town, you'll find the **Collégiale Notre-Dame-des-Anges**, a 17th-century church. Its Baroque interior is filled with gilded statues, frescoes and faux marble. Parts of the church date back to the 12th century. *Info: Center of Old Town. Open daily. Admission: Free.*

Next to the Collégiale Notre-Dame-des-Anges on the place de la Liberté is the picturesque **Café de France**, a good place for a break.

This otherwise quiet town is filled with crowds on Sunday. Stands loaded with local produce, crafts and antiques fill the streets along with street performers. There's a more sedate market on Thursdays. *Info: From the place Gambetta (the main entrance to the town) up avenue des 4 Otages.*

L'ISLE-SUR-LA-SORGUE SLEEPS & EATS
Hostellerie la Grangette €€-€€€

There's lots of charm at this peaceful, vine-covered inn surrounded by oak trees just three miles north of L'Isle-sur-la-Sorgue in the town of Velleron. Fantastic pool. Rooms have tiled floors and are tastefully decorated with antiques from the markets in L'Isle-sur-la-Sorgue. Excellent lunch or dinner on the terrace (reservations required). Note temporarily closed at time of press until mid-2016. *Info: Chemin Cambuisson in Velleron. Tel. 04/90.20.00.77. V, MC. Restaurant, outdoor pool, telephone, wireless Internet access. Closed mid-Nov to mid-Feb.*

La Bastide Rose €€-€€€
This pink villa is located next to a canal. There's a wonderful pool, river views, and an old mill turned into the Pierre Salinger Museum (the owner used to be married to JFK's press secretary). There are five rooms (all have large bathrooms), two suites and a cottage for rent. *Info: 99 Chemin des Croupières in Le Thor (just outside of town). www.bastiderose.com. Tel. 04/90.02.14.33. V, MC, AE. Restaurant, AC, TV, telephone, minibar, in-room safe, hairdryer, WiFi.*

The attractive **restaurant** here is open every evening and Sunday for lunch from Apr-Oct. Closed Tue (except in Jul and Aug). Menus start at €35.

Le Café du Village-€€

This café and restaurant is located in one of the largest and oldest antique centers in the city. Have a light lunch and sip a glass of wine from the Luberon region on the shaded terrace. You'll be surrounded by vendors and shoppers. Just the type of dining experience you came to Provence for. *Info: 2 bis ave. de l'égalité. www.lecafeduvillage.fr. Tel. 04/90.15.47.49. Open at noon Mon-Fr.*

Le Jardin du Quai €€€

This popular restaurant serves innovative dishes. In good weather, you can dine in its large and lovely garden under chestnut trees. Friendly service. Order the tasty *filet de boeuf* (beef tenderloin). The restaurant also offers cooking classes and has a small shop selling local food specialties and Luberon wines. *Info: 91 avenue Julien Guigue (opposite the station). www.jardin-du-quai.com. Tel. 04/90.20.14.98. Closed Tue and Wed.*

La Prévôte €€€

Splurge on award-winning cuisine in a lovely setting on a narrow street near the cathedral. Try the excellent *rable de lapin farcis au chèvre* (loin of rabbit stuffed with goat cheese). *Info: 4 bis rue Jean-Jacques-Rousseau. www.la-prevote.fr. Tel. 04/90.38.57.29. Closed Tue (year round) and Wed (Sep-Jun).*

The chic **inn** (€€-€€€) here offers five rooms decorated with interesting antiques (which is fitting for this town known for its antique shops). *Info: 4 bis rue Jean-Jacques-Rousseau. www.la-prevote.fr. Tel. 04/90.38.57.29. V, MC. AC, TV, telephone, safe, WiFi.*

Le Caveau de la Tour de l'Isle €-€€
A popular wine bar and store on the cobblestone, pedestrian-only street leading to the cathedral. You can try wines by the glass with local cheese and sausage. *Info: 12 rue de la République. Tel. 04/90.20.70.25. Closed Mon and Tue.*

FONTAINE-DE-VAUCLUSE
While nearby L'Isle-sur-la-Sorgue has been called the "Venice of Provence," **Fontaine-de-Vaucluse** has been called the "Niagara Falls of Provence." It's 5 miles (8 km) east of L'Isle-sur-la-Sorgue/20 miles (32 km) east of Avignon. Parking €3-€4 on both sides of town.

Don't be fooled, though, as at times of the year the *fontaine*, in a cave at the end of a riverside walk, is not much to look at. Europe's most powerful spring gushes 55 million gallons of water each day from the base of 750-feet-high cliffs. The source? No one really knows. Millions visit this sight, and the little village of the same name is loaded with souvenir shops and cafés. You'll pass these on your way to the *fontaine* after you pay to park your car. Visit early or late in the day to avoid the crowds. In the evening, the illuminated *château* sparkles above the town.

While here, there are plenty of cafés and restaurants to take a break. There are also several good special-interest museums.

The **Musée d'Histoire 1939-1945** is a modern museum devoted to the literature, art and history of World War II, especially the Nazi occupation of France. *Info: chemin de la Fontaine. Tel. 04/90.20.24.00. Closed Tue and Dec 25-May 1. Admission: €4.*

The small **Musée Pétrarque** honors Petrarch, an Italian Renaissance poet who moved here after being rejected by a married woman. *Info: Rive Gauche de la Sorgue (village center). Tel. 04/90.20.58.36. Closed Tue and Nov-Mar. Admission: €4.*

Moulin Vallis-Clausa is a working paper mill where artisans create paper as done in the 15th-century. *Info: chemin de la Fontaine. Tel. 04/90.20.34.14. Open daily 10am-6pm. Admission: Free.*

Guided canoe trips depart from Fontaine-de-Vaucluse on two-hour, five-mile trips down the Sorgue River. The trip ends in nearby L'Isle-sur-la-Sorgue and a shuttle brings you back. There are several tour companies offering these trips. One is **Kayaks Verts,** *Tel. 04/90.20.35.44, €20.*

GORDES & THE VILLAGE DES BORIES
Perched above the Coulon Valley, the small picturesque village of **Gordes** has narrow alleys between stone homes that appear to be stacked on top of each other. It's 10 miles (16 km) southeast of Fontaine-de-Vaucluse/22 miles (36 km) east of Avignon. Gordes is touristy and trendy, with boutiques and galleries.

In the center of town, you'll find the fortified Renaissance **Château des Gordes.** You can view its interior, with its winding staircases. a

beautifully carved fireplace dating from 1541, and a contemporary art collection. *Info: Center of town. Tel. 04/90.72.98.64. Open daily. Admission: €5.*

Also in the center of town is the **Eglise St-Fermin**. Stop in for a quick view of the church's blue floral interior and faux marble pulpit. *Info: Center of town. Open daily. Admission: Free.*

Only two miles away from Gordes is a popular tourist destination, the **Village des Bories**. *Bories* are beehive-shaped stone huts built by peasants (without mortar) who lived in them while tending their flocks. There are said to be 6,000 in Provence. It's believed that Neolithic man lived in huts like these, and that they were copied over the years. This cluster of *bories* is part of a village showcasing this peasant community, which was inhabited between 1600 and 1800. Note that if you're unable to park in the lot closest to the village, the walk from route D2 is 1.2 miles (2 km). *Info: 2 miles (4 km) southwest of Gordes off route D2 toward Coustellet. Tel. 04/90.72.03.48. Open daily 9am until sunset. Admission: €6.*

GORDES SLEEPS & EATS
La Bastide €€-€€€
This 45-unit inn – suites are the most expensive – is located in one of the stone homes that appear to be stacked on top of each other here. Tastefully decorated rooms, attentive staff, and a luxurious pool all make this a perfect base to explore the area.

Info: Le Village. www.bastide-de-gordes.com. Tel. 04/90.72.12.12. V, MC, DC, AE. Restaurant, bar, gym, AC, TV, telephone, minibar, in-room safe, hairdryer, WiFi.

The **restaurant** here (€€€) serves Provençal and Mediterranean dishes on the lovely terrace. Attentive staff. *Info: Le Village. Tel. 04/90.72.12.12. www.bastide-de-gordes.com. Fixed-priced menu. Open daily for lunch and dinner.*

Les Cuisines du Château €€
This small, 1930s-style bistro serves wonderful roast meats (especially lamb). Garlic *aïoli* (mayonnaise), a Provençal specialty, is featured
in many dishes. *Info: place du Château (across from the château). Tel.
04/90.72.01.31. Closed Tue (dinner) and Wed. Closed mid-Nov to mid-Dec.*

Only two miles from Gordes is
a must-see sight and worth the
drive, especially if you're visiting
in late June, July or August, when
the lavender fields surrounding
the austere 12th-century abbey
**Abbaye Notre-Dame de Sé-
nanque** are in splendid bloom.
Even if you don't visit the abbey,
don't miss this perfect photo op-
portunity. You can visit he cloisters, church, refectory and dormitory. The only heated room was
the calefactory, or sitting room,
which allowed the monks to read
and write without freezing. There
are permanent exhibits on the
history of the Cistercians and the
construction of the abbey, and there are still monks who make this
their home. *Info: 2 miles (4 km) north of Gordes on route D177. www.
senanque.fr. Tel. 04/90.72.05.86. Open Mon-Sat 9:45am-11am. Admission:
€7.50 (unguided tour).*

ROUSSILLON
We'll visit colorful **Roussillon** and experience a taste of old Provence
in **Oppède-le-Vieux**. Roussillon is 6 miles (10 km) east of Gordes/28
miles (45 km) east of Avignon.

Legend has it that a local lord had his wife's lover killed and the wife
threw herself off a cliff, staining the rocks with her blood. In real-
ity, two centuries of ochre mining have left this perched village surrounded by red quarries and cliffs. From deep red to light yellow, the
colors of this town alone are worth a visit. Although it can be quite
crowded in high tourist season, you can still find peaceful, beautiful

squares and take in the surrounding countryside.

The Sentier des Ocres (Ochre Trail)

Two circular trails (30 minutes and 50 minutes) in the village have signs that highlight local flora and the history of ochre mining. The peaceful walks take you through chestnut and pine groves. *Info: 9:30am-5:30pm. Admission: €3.*

Domaine de Tara

Located less than a mile northwest of Roussillon, this winery has a tasting room where you can sample wines from its vineyard. Lovely setting facing the Monts du Vaucluse, Mont Ventoux and the village of Gordes. *Info: Les Rossignols. Off of D102 on the road to Joucas. www.domaine-detara.com. Tel. 04/90.05.74.87. Open daily 10am-7:30pm.*

COLORFUL LAVENDER

It's everywhere and it's beautiful. During **lavender season** (late June through August), there's nothing more breathtaking than lavender fields and yellow fields of sunflowers. Lavender is harvested beginning in July and distilled for perfume and soap. Some of the most spectacular lavender fields are found between Buoux and Forcalquier. For those interested in lavender, you can visit the **Musée de la Lavande** on route D2 in Cabrières outside of Gordes. *Info: www.museedelalavande.com. Tel. 04/90.76.91.23. Open daily. Admission: €7 (includes English audioguide).*

ROUSSILLON SLEEPS& EATS

Le Clos de la Glycine €€

Located in the heart of the village, this comfortable nine-room inn is a great choice. Rooms are charming and most have sweeping views of the ochre cliffs. *Info: place de la Poste. www.luberon-hotel.fr. Tel. 04/90.05.60.13. V, MC. AC, TV, minibar, safe, hairdryer, WiFi.*

Restaurant David €€

Provençal specialties are served at this attractive restaurant located at Le Clos de la Glycine inn (*see above*) in the heart of Roussillon. The restaurant has panoramic views and a terrace overlooking the ochre cliffs. Dinner menus start at €33. Try the *filet d'agneau de pays rôti* (roasted baked lamb filet). *Info: place de la Poste. www.luberon-hotel. fr. Tel. 04/90.05.60.13.*

Le Bistro de Roussillon €€
Indoor and outdoor dining at this friendly bistro serving hearty Provençal fare. You'll enjoy the view of the countryside from the terrace on the charming little square. *Info: place de la Marine. Tel. 04/90.05.74.45. Closed Jan and mid-Nov to mid-Dec.*

Just three miles (five km) southeast of Roussillon on route D108 is the **Pont Julien**. This three-arched bridge was built by the Romans over 2000 years ago without the use of mortar. It crosses the Calavon River.

While Roussillon is usually crowded with tourists, the nearby town of **Oppède-le-Vieux** will give you a taste of Old Provence. It's 9 miles (14 km) south of Gordes/16 miles (26 km) southeast of Avignon.

This hilltop village (don't confuse it with the lower modern town of Oppède), surrounded by thick forests, was deserted in 1900. The ruins of a medieval *château* loom above. In fact, much of the town itself is still in ruins, although some artists and writers have moved in and beautifully restored homes. You must park at the base of the hill (€3) and walk through a tiered garden filled with local plants labeled with their Latin, French and English names. Cross through the old city gate and walk up the steep alleys to visit the 13th-century church **Notre-Dame d'Alydon**, with its gargoyles and hexagon-shaped bell tower. Truly a taste of old Provence.

Outside of the old city gate are two places to stop for a drink or a bite. **Le Petit Café** and **L'Echauguette** both have decent fare at reasonable prices.

MÉNERBES & THE LAND OF A YEAR IN PROVENCE

Peter Mayle wrote *A Year in Provence* about **Ménerbes** and the towns surrounding it. Ménerbes is 3 miles (5 km) east of Oppède-le-Vieux/19 miles (31 km) southeast of Avignon.

This town with its impressive fortifications and crowned by the turreted *château* was once a Protestant stronghold during the 16th-century War of the Religions. You'll find Renaissance homes and terrific views of the countryside. Visit the attractive **Place de l'Horloge** (Clock Square), in the shadow of City Hall.

Although Picasso once owned a home in Ménerbes, it's another home that gets all the attention. Peter Mayle wrote the enormously successful *A Year in Provence* about his home and the towns surrounding it. Tour buses still pass by and gawk. He no longer lives here and it's hard to feel sorry for the current owners as they must have known what they were getting themselves into! *Info: 1 mile (2 km) from Ménerbes on route D3 to Bonnieux (second house from the right after the soccer field). No admission.*

Between Oppède-le-Vieux and Ménerbes is the **Musée du Tire-Bouchon** (Corkscrew Museum). Housed in a mansion, this museum doesn't just feature thousands of corkscrews. It also has wine tastings. *Info: On route D109 between Oppède-le-Vieux and Ménerbes. Tel. 04/90.72.41.58. Closed Sun in winter. Admission: €4.*

Just four miles (six km) east of Ménerbes is **Lacoste**. This town with its fortified medieval gateways is dominated by the *château* that was once owned by the Marquis de Sade who hosted his infamous orgies here. The castle is currently being restored by designer Pierre Cardin. The town comes to life in July and August when the **Festival Lacoste**, with musical and theatrical events, takes place.

When visiting this area, don't miss the hilltop village of **Bonnieux**. It's 3 miles (5km) east of Lacoste/7 miles (11 km) southeast of Rousillon/28 miles (46 km) northwest of Aix-en-Provence.

Layers of homes topped with a 12th-century church (the simply named **Vieille Eglise** or "Old Church") make Bonnieux one of the most impressive hilltop villages. Its steep streets are bordered by restored homes. Climb the 86 steps from the place de la Liberté and rue de la Mairie up to the church to take in the great view of the surrounding countryside.

There's nothing like French bread. The **Musée de la Boulangerie**, in a 17th-century house, features a century-old bread oven and bread shop. Exhibits show all phases of breadmaking. *Info: 12 rue de la République. Tel. 04/90.75.88.34. Open 10am-noon and 2pm-6pm.Closed Tue and Nov-Mar. Admission: €4.*

BONNIEUX SLEEPS & EATS

Maison de l'Aiguebrun €€

You'll find seven rooms and four cabins at this farmhouse/inn located in a small valley near Bonnieux. Relax at the comfortable pool surrounded by lush gardens. *Info: 4 miles (6 km) southeast of Bonnieux (near the intersection of routes D36 and D943). www.maisondelaiguebrun. com. Tel. 04/90.04.47.00. TV, DVD, telephone, hairdryer, WiFi.*

The **restauran**t here (€€-€€€) serves Provençal cuisine on an attractive terrace. Reservations required for dinner.

Le Fournil €€

Dine outdoors by the 12th-century fountain or inside in a grotto at

this former bakery. Provençal cuisine and a great wine list. Try the *longe de veau* (veal loin) or the *suprême de pintade aux morilles* (guinea fowl with morel mushrooms). *Info: 5 place Carnot. www. lefournil-bonnieux.com. Tel. 90.75.83.62. Closed Mon, Sat (lunch), Dec, Jan to mid-Feb and mid-Nov to mid-Dec.*

If you want to visit one of Peter Mayle's favorites from his famous book, head to the small town of **Buoux**, five miles (nine km) south of Apt. This peaceful rural town is surrounded by lavender fields and crowned by the ruins of the Buoux Fort. It's a destination for the popular Auberge de la Loube restaurant (*see next page*).

BUOUX EATS
Auberge de la Loube €€€
This restaurant gained renown in Peter Mayle's *A Year in Provence*. The Provençal fare won't disappoint, especially the *agneau rôti* (roast lamb). Dining is on the comfortable covered patio. *Info: Quartier la Loube. Tel. 04/90.74.19.58. Closed Wed, Thu and Jan.*

APT & SAIGNON
Apt is 32 miles (52 km) northwest of Aix-en-Provence/32 miles (52 km) west of Avignon.

Apt's claim to fame, despite its unattractive industrial outskirts, is that it's the world capital of *fruits-confits* (candied fruit). You'll find shops selling it everywhere. The **Vieille Ville** (Old Town) with its narrow streets is worth a visit. The **Cathédrale St-Anne** (closed Sunday afternoons) in the Old Town has a large collection of relics (guided tours only), and the cathedral's crypt is said to hold the remains of St. Anne, the mother of the Virgin Mary.

There's a huge market on Saturday mornings at place de la Bouquerie. Especially good for purchasing *fruits-confits* (candied fruit), for which the town is known.

Nearby is the truly unspoiled hill town of **Saignon**. It's two miles (three km) southeast of Apt. Out of the way, but certainly worth the trip! This lovely, quiet, and unspoiled town high on a hill has picturesque shady squares, time-worn fountains and ruins of ancient baths. The wood-carved doors of the Roman church **Eglise Notre-Dame de Pitié** depict Christ and Mary. The cemetery behind the church provides its permanent "residents" with a panoramic view of the countryside.

SAIGNON SLEEPS
Chambre Avec Vue €-€€
This lovely bed and breakfast is located in an 18th-century building in the center of this unspoiled town. The rooms – several with terraces – have been recently renovated. Hospitable owners. This place is a favorite with artists and you'll find contemporary art on every wall. Breakfast (included) is served in the tranquil garden. Walkers and hikers will enjoy the nearby trails. *Info: Rue des Bourgades. www.chambreavecvue.com. Tel. 04/90.04.85.01. V, MC. Studios include kitchenettes.*

LOURMARIN
Hungry? Head to **Lourmarin**, the gastronomic capital of Provence. It's six miles (ten km) south of Bonnieux.

Lourmarin's winding narrow streets are lined with stone houses painted in shades of ochre and beige. It has a Renaissance chapel and both Catholic and Protestant churches. The village lies at the foot of the Luberon Mountain range which is covered with pine and oak trees. Surrounding the village are olive groves and vineyards. Although French vacationers discovered this little village years ago, it's now popular with foreign tourists. Its renovated *château* is the site of frequent concerts and exhibits. Visitors have quite a few cafés and restaurants to choose from, and it's become the gastronomic capital of the area. It's a lovely town with much to offer, and a great base for touring some of the prettiest towns of Provence.

There's a **Friday-morning market** in Lourmarin.

When in town, head to **La Cave à Lourmarin**. The interesting wines of the Côtes du Luberon, along with regional products, are available at incredibly discounted prices at this shop in the center of town. Friendly and helpful staff and generous wine tastings. *Info: Montée du Galinier. Tel. 04/90.68.02.18. Open daily.*

LOURMARIN SLEEPS & EATS
Les Olivettes €€
Les Olivettes offers private apartments in a newly renovated farmhouse in the Luberon. It has spectacular views, a large heated swimming-pool, private gardens and, most of all, a relaxing and peaceful atmosphere. English-speaking Joe and Elisabeth Deliso are the perfect

hosts. It's an ideal base for visiting the villages of the Luberon. *Info: Ave. Henri Bosco (off of route 27). www.olivettes.com. Tel. 04/90.68.03.52. Weekly rentals. V, MC. Outdoor pool. Kitchens, TV, telephone, minibar, WiFi. Closed Dec-Feb. Weekly rentals required in high season.*

Le Moulin €€-€€€

This hotel is located in a 17th-century building. The 17 rooms and 2 suites are decorated with local pottery and Provençal furniture. You can relax in the attractive lounge near the fireplace or on the terrace. *Info: rue du Temple. www.moulindelourmarin.com. Tel. 04/90.68.06.69. V, MC. Each room has different amenities, including AC, TV, minibar, safe, hairdryer. Wifi available in common areas.*

The **restaurant** here (€€-€€€) serves French and Provençal dishes. Try the *côte de veau* (veal chop) served in a sage sauce. You'll dine in a lovely room with vaulted ceilings and stone walls. *Info: Closed Mon.*

Le Comptoir 2 Michel-Ange €€

This café and restaurant serves Italian and Provençal dishes on a lovely square in the middle of town. An excellent place to have a light lunch and sip a glass of local rosé. Try the delicious *fleurs des courgettes farcie*s (zucchini flowers stuffed with cheese). *Info: place Barthlémy/ Monté du Galnier. Tel. 04/90.08.49.13. Closed Wed.*

Auberge La Fenière €€€

Chef Reine Sammut is called the "Queen of Provençal cooking." Experience her innovative dishes at this restaurant on the outskirts of town. *Info: Route de Ca-* denet (D943). www.reinesammut.com. Tel. 04/90.68.11.79. Open daily in high season.*

The **inn** here (€€-€€€) has stylish rooms housed in several different buildings on the estate. Lush gardens and a beautiful pool! *Info: AC, TV, WiFi, parking.*

MOST BEAUTIFUL VILLAGES

There are 141 villages throughout France designated as **Plus Beaux Villages** (Most Beautiful Villages). In order to receive this designation, the village must have a population under 2,000 and have at least two sites or buildings designated as "protected" by the government. The villages featured in this book are: Moustiers-Ste-Marie, Gourdon, Les Baux-de-Provence, Ansouis, Gordes, Lourmarin, Ménerbes, Roussillon, Séguret, and Gassin.

There are two towns nearby that are worth the short drives. **Cucuron** (*see photo on next page*) is only four miles (seven km) east of Lourmarin. Tourism has yet to invade this scenic small town. Parts of the ancient walls survive. A fortified gate and bell tower on place de l'Horloge is the entry for the ruins above the town. Take a break with locals at cafés along the **Bassin de l'Etang** (a large stone pool) dating back to the 15th century. There's a large market here on Tuesday mornings. The church **Eglise Notre-Dame-de-Beaulieu** has Gothic chapels and a Baroque altarpiece. Near the church is an ancient olive press, **Moulin à Huile Dauphin**, with a shop selling local specialties.

Ansouis is only eight miles (ten km) southeast of Lourmarin; the town lies at the foot of its **medieval castle**. The village houses are spread over the southern slope to shelter them from the *Mistral* (the brutal winds that touch this area at certain times of the year). There's a 16th-century tower crowned with a wrought-iron bell tower, and the castle with its fortified walls and watchtower has been restored (guided visits only in the afternoons). Wooded groves, gardens and terraces surround the castle. You can pop into the church **Eglise St-Martin**. Originally a 12th-century fortress and former law court, this small church contains 17th- and 18th-century statues and altar pieces. At the entry to the castle, you can stop into the information center and purchase an inexpensive bottle of local wine.

Gardeners must visit **La Ferme de Gerbaud**, a 62-acre farm on the slopes of the Luberon mountain range offering 90-minute guided tours in English and French. You'll see aromatic herbs and regional plants. The shop sells fragrances, dyes, olive oils and herbs. *Info: 2 miles (3 km) outside of Lourmarin (chemin d'Aguye to chemin de Gerbaud). Tel. 04/90.68.11.83. Tours Apr-Oct Tue, Thu and Sat at 5pm, Nov-Mar Sun at 3pm. Admission: €5.*

9. Aix-en-Provence

HIGHLIGHTS

• A walk down the cours Mirabeau, Aix's lovely main street

• Quartier Mazarin, filled with elegant townhouses

• The huge market at place Verdun

• Musée Granet/Musée des Beaux-Arts, home to eight Cézanne paintings

INTRO

Aix (pronounced "X") is a graceful and sophisticated city. Between the 12th and 15th centuries it was the capital of Provence. The Romans called it "Aquae Sextius" (Waters of Sextius) after the thermal springs that flow here and the Roman general (Caius Sextius Calvinus) who founded the city.

Shaded squares with bubbling fountains in the Old Quarter, 17th-century town houses and the **cours Mirabeau** (the grand main avenue) make Aix a must for all visitors to Provence. It's a cultural center enhanced by thousands of students who attend one of France's oldest universities. It's the hometown of the artist **Paul Cézanne**, who created many of his best-known works here.

COORDINATES

Aix-en-Provence (population 130,000) is in the south of France. It's 19 miles (31km) northeast of the Mediterranean port city of Marseille, 51 miles (82km) southeast of Avignon, and 474 miles (760km) south of Paris. The tourist office and parking areas are at place Général-de-Gaulle. Aix-en-Provence has a TGV (fast-speed train) station on the edge of town. For more information on train travel to Aix, see the Practical Matters section.

SIGHTS

La Rotonde

The black and-white **marble fountain** at place Général-de-Gaulle (in the middle of the traffic circle) dates back to the 19th century, and features the figures of Fine Art, Agriculture and Justice at the top.

cours Mirabeau

This broad street lined with plane trees and stone buildings was built in the 17th century. You'll pass elegant buildings, four fountains, and many cafés and shops. This is the heart of Aix. One of the grand mansions on this street, the impressive

Hôtel Maurel de Pontèves (now the Tribunal of Commerce, *photo above*) with its sculpted figures is at number 38. In the middle of the cours Mirabeau is the **Fontaine Moussue** (it means "Mossy Fountain" – you'll understand why when you see it). The formal name of this fountain is **Fontaine d'Eau Chaude** (Hot Water Fountain).

Quartier Mazarin

It was here that Aix nobility built elegant town houses in the 17th and 18th centuries. **Place des Quatre Dauphins** is dominated by a Ba-

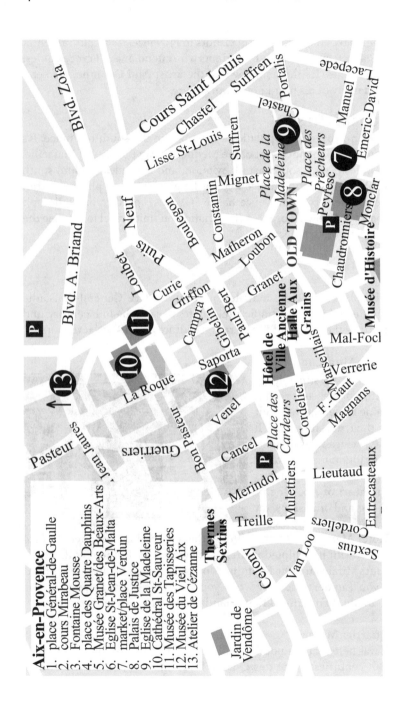

Aix-en-Provence
1. place Général-de-Gaulle
2. cours Mirabeau
3. Fontaine Mousse
4. place des Quatre Dauphins
5. Musée Granet/des Beaux-Arts
6. Eglise St-Jean-de-Malta
7. market/place Verdun
8. Palais de Justice
9. Eglise de la Madeleine
10. Cathédral St-Sauveur
11. Musée des Tapisseries
12. Musée du Vieil Aix
13. Atelier de Cézanne

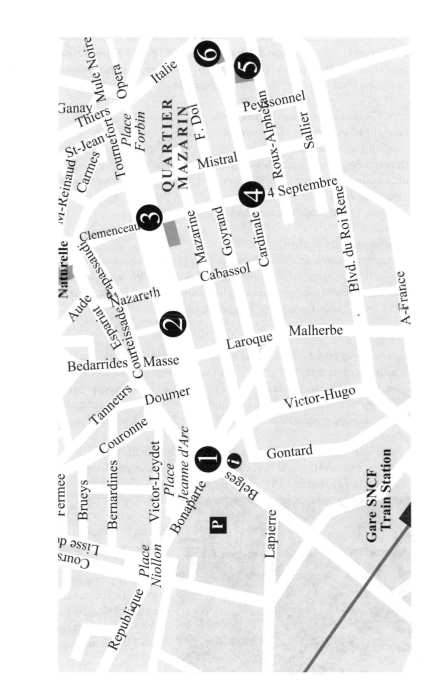

roque fountain. The elegant 17th-century **Fontaine des Quatre Dauphins** (Four Dolphins Fountain) features four dolphins at the base of a pine cone-topped obelisk. *Info: If you exit the cours Mirabeau onto rue du 4 Septembre, you'll enter the Quartier Mazarin.*

Musée Granet/Musée des Beaux-Arts

One sight of interest in the Quartier Mazarin is located in a former priory and is home to a collection of European art from the 16th to 19th centuries. You'll find at least eight **Cézanne** paintings here, along with a collection of his drawings and watercolors. *Info: place St-Jean-de-Malte on rue Cardinale. Tel. 04/42.52.88.32. Open noon-6pm (Jul-Oct until 7pm). Closed Mon. Admission: €5.*

Eglise St-Jean-de-Malte

This Gothic church and chapel of the Knights of Malta (a charitable organization) is home to the tombs of the counts of Provence. Drop in for a quick view. It's located next to the Musée Granet. *Info: rue Cardinale and rue d'Italie. Open daily. Admission: Free.*

place Verdun

This square in Old Town is home to the grand **Palais de Justice** (Palace of Justice), completed in 1831. On the adjoining place des Prêcheurs is the **Eglise de la Madeleine**. Formerly a Dominican convent, this Baroque church is the site of frequent classical concerts. *Info: place des Prêcheurs (off of place de la Madeleine). Open daily. Admission: Free.*

If you're here on Tuesday, Thursday or Saturday mornings, you'll run into a huge **market**. You'll find clothes, antiques and produce at the colorful **Aix Market** held in place de Verdun and place des Prêch-

eurs. From place Verdun, you'll find the **Passage Agard** (it has the word "Agard" written above it). It's a covered passageway lined with shops. The *passage* connects the place Verdun with the cours Mirabeau.

Cathédral St-Sauveur

On the rue Gaston-de-Saporta (the heart of Old Town), this cathedral has a 5th-century baptistery, 12th-century cloisters and a 15th-century triptych (three-paneled painting), *The Burning Bush*. The famous triptych is only open for special occasions, however, to protect it from further deterioration. Near the triptych is another three-paneled painting of Christ's passion. The fantastic gilt organ is Baroque, and the tapestries surrounding the choir date from the 18th century. *Info: rue Gaston-de-Saporta at place des Martyrs de la Résistance. Admission: Free.*

Musée des Tapisseries

This 17th-century archbishop's palace is home to a museum of 17th- and 18th-century tapestries and furnishings. It's located next to the cathedral. *Info: 28 place des Martyrs de la Résistance. Tel. 04/42.23.09.91. Open Feb-Apr 14 and Oct 16-Dec 31 1:30pm-5pm. Open April 15-Oct 15 10am-12:30pm and 1:30pm-6pm. Closed Tue and Jan. Admission: €3.50.*

Musée Estienne de Saint-Jean/Musée du Vieil Aix

This beautiful 17th-century mansion is more interesting than the museum of eclectic furniture and objects it houses. *Info: 17 rue Gaston-de-Saporta. Tel. 04/42.21.43.55. Open 10am-12:30pm and 1:30pm-6pm (Oct-Mar until 5pm). Closed Tue. Admission: Free.*

Atelier de Cézanne

The artist Paul Cézanne is from Aix, and created many of his best-known works here. You can visit his studio, the **Atelier de Cézanne**. It's located just north of the Old Town. Cézanne painted some of his best-known works here. Americans paid to have his studio restored, and you'll find it much like he left it in 1906. *Info: 9 avenue Paul-Cézanne. www.atelier-cezanne.com. Tel. 04/42.21.06.53. Open daily Apr-Jun and Sep 10am-noon and 2pm-6pm, Jul and Aug 10am-6pm, Oct-Mar 10am-noon and 2pm-5pm. Tours in English at 4pm (Oct-Mar) and 5pm (Apr-Sep. Closed Sun Dec-Feb. Admission: €6.*

If you chose to head out of town, you might want to visit **Meyrargues** (11 miles (19 km) northeast of Aix-en-Provence). This village was a Celtic outpost in 600 B.C. It's dominated by a fortress that was transformed into a *château* in the 17th century and then into an 11-room luxury hotel in the 1950s. Most come to stay at the castle/hotel. They won't mind if you look around the castle and its grounds. The village is charming (despite some bad 1960s apartment buildings in one section). You'll find sweeping views from the castle, along with the remains of a Roman aqueduct in the valley below. *Info: Château de Meyragues, www.chateau-de-meyrargues.com.*

BEST SLEEPS & EATS

Hotel Cézanne €€€

This modern, chic hotel has fun and eclectic décor. There are 55 rooms and 12 suites. Its location near the train station makes it a great place to stay if you plan to venture out to other towns in Provence. Tasty, large brunch is served daily. The only thing it lacks is a pool. *Info: 40 ave. Victor Hugo. www.cezanne.hotelaix.com. Tel. 04/42.91.11.11. V, MC, AE. Bar, AC, TV, telephone, minibar, safe, WiFi.*

Villa Gallici €€€

A stylish and sumptuous hotel located in a garden just a short walk from the cours Mirabeau. Many of the 22 rooms have their own pati-

os. Pleasant outdoor pool. *Info: avenue de la Violette. Tel. 04/42.23.29.23. www.villagallici.com. V, MC, DC, AE. Restaurant, bar, AC, TV, telephone, minibar, safe, WiFi.*

Grand Hôtel Nègre Coste €-€€

Smack dab in the middle of the cours Mirabeau, this traditional hotel is a little faded, but certainly worth considering. Rooms are medium-sized and have soundproof windows. Some have great views of the cours Mirabeau, Aix's main street. *Info: 33 cours Mirabeau. www.hotel-negrecoste.com. Tel. 04/42.27.74.22. V, MC, AE. AC, TV, minibar, hairdyer, safe.*

Hôtel Cardinal €

Located in the Quartier Mazarin filled with elegant town houses, this 29-room hotel (and nearby annex) is a good value with basic, comfortable rooms, a helpful staff and a great location. Note that with no air-conditioning, rooms can be hot in summer. *Info: 24 rue Cardinale. www.hotel-cardinal-aix.com. Tel. 04/42.38.32.30. V, MC. TV, hairdyer.*

Hôtel des Quatre Dauphins €-€€

Also located in the quiet Quartier Mazarin, this small, 13-room hotel is another good value with basic, comfortable accommodations and a great location. *Info: 54 rue Roux-Alphéran. www.lesquatredauphins.fr. Tel. 04/42.38.16.39. V, MC. TV.*

La Fromagerie du Passage €€

This restaurant, wine shop, and cheese shop is located in the Passage Agard (a covered passageway that connects place Verdun with the cours Mirabeau). The highlight here is "Le Tour de France" a cheese platter paired with Provençal wines for €24. This is also a great place for lunch as they serve excellent sandwiches (most of which are under €7). You can dine on the rooftop terrace. *Info: Passage Agard/55 cours Mirabeau. www.lafromageriedupassage.fr. Tel. 04/42.22.90.00. Open daily.*

Le Saint-Estève €€€

This award-winning restaurant is located at the Hôtel Les Lodges Sainte-Victoire (€€€). Both the restaurant and hotel opened in 2013 on ten acres about a ten-minute drive from Aix. You'll dine on chef Mathias Dandine's innovative French cuisine with a view of the surrounding vineyards, olive groves, and mountains. This is one of Provence

and the French Riviera's best places to dine. *Info: 2250 route de Cézanne in Le Tholonet. www.leslodgessaintevictoire.com. Tel. 04/42.27.10.14. Reservations required. Fixed-price lunch from €45. Fixed-priced dinner from €85. Closed Mon.*

L'Épicurien €€
This small bistro in the Old Town serves Provençal cuisine with an emphasis on fresh fish, meat, and produce from local markets. You'll order from the blackboard menu that changes frequently. Friendly service. *Info: 13 place des Cardeurs. Tel. 06/89.33.49.83. Closed Sun and Mon.*

Mitch €€-€€€
Innovative cuisine served in a stone-walled restaurant and on the patio. One of our favorites! Try the pan-fried *Saint-Jacques* (sea scallops) or the *magret de canard* (duck breast) served in a sweet-and-sour sauce. End your meal with the *cylinder au citron*, a lemon pastry. *Info: 26 rue des Tanneurs (at avenue Aumône Vieille). Tel. 04/42.26.63.08. Closed Sun.*

Brasserie Les Deux Garçons €€
This 19th-century *brasserie* has waiters in aprons, a beautiful interior and great people-watching from its sidewalk tables along the cours Mirabeau. Standard *brasserie* fare. *Info: 53 cours Mirabeau. www.les-2garcons.fr. Tel. 04/42.26.00.51. Open daily.*

BEST SHOPPING
Aix is one of the best cities in Provence to shop. You'll find fashionable clothing shops (especially on **rue Fabrot**), Provençal fabric shops (**Les Olivades** at 15 rue Marius Reinaud), and shops selling *calissons d'Aix*, a candy made from ground almonds, melon, and fruit syrup (**Béchard** at 12 cours Mirabeau).

BEST NIGHTLIFE & ENTERTAINMENT
Scat Club
Late-night jazz, blues, rock and world-music performances. *Info: 11 rue de la Verrerie. Tel.04/42.23.00.23.*

Casino Aix
If you're tired of museums and cafés, try your luck at the casino. There are also five restaurants here. *Info: 21 ave. de l'Europe. www.ca-*

sinoaix.com. Tel. 04/. 42.59.69.00. Open daily. Slot machines from 10am. Gaming tables from 3pm.

Le Mistral
The most popular dance club in Aix, filled with university students. You'll need to dress up to get in. *Info: 3 rue Frédéric-Mistral. www.mistralclub.fr. Tel. 06/74.63.04.92. Closed most Mon and Sun.*

Aix has several **gay and gay-friendly** establishments:
*   **Cha Do**, *46 cours Sextus, Tel. 04/42.27.70.63 (bar)*
*   **Happy Days**, *place Richelieu, Tel. 04/42.21.02.35 (bar)*
*   **Aix Sauna Club**, *8 bis rue Annonerie Vieille, Tel. 04/42.27.21.49.*

Festival d'Aix is held in late June and early July. World-class opera productions are held in the courtyard of the Palais de l'Archevêché and other venues throughout the city. *Info: www.festival-aix.com.*

BEST SPORTS & RECREATION
Le Golf de la Sainte Victoire
Designed by Robert Trent Jones, this prestigious golf club is located in nearby Fuveau, only 7 miles (12km) from Aix. *Info: Chemin Maurel in Fuveau (route D6). Tel. 04/42.29.83.43.*

10. Arles

HIGHLIGHTS
• Espace Van Gogh, Roman ruins

• Old Town in St. Rémy

• Les Baux de Provence, a delightful medieval hilltop village with great views

• Flamingos and birds in the Parc Regional de Camargue

INTRO
On the banks of the Rhône River, **Arles** is one of the three "A's" that make up the most visited cities in Provence (along with Aix-en-Provence and Avignon). Arles has everything you could want in a Provence city: festivals, an Old Town, Roman ruins, cafés (especially on **place du Forum**) and intimate restaurants.

Since Arles is situated at the head of the Rhône delta, it's on the route that linked Italy and Spain. When the Romans came into possession of Spain, Arles became an important and strategic town for them.

Bullfights, still held in the arena, are a reminder of Arles's Spanish connection. The folk culture and traditions of Arles are alive and well, and you'll see locals dressed in traditional Arlesian costumes on many occasions. **Van Gogh** came here in 1888 and created some of his best-known paintings. Look around and you'll notice that many of the scenes featured in those paintings remain today.

COORDINATES

Arles (population 50,000) is in the south of France. It's 57 miles (92km) inland from the Mediterranean port city of Marseille, 22 miles (36km) south of Avignon, and 450 miles (752km) south of Paris. Arles can be reached from Avignon by bus (60 minutes) and by train (20 minutes). The train station and bus station in Arles are now located next to each other.

SIGHTS

Espace van Gogh

This is where Vincent van Gogh was sent after he is said to have cut off part of his left ear. The courtyard, which is open to the public, has been landscaped to match van Gogh's famous painting *Le Jardin de l'Hôtel-Dieu*. The building was formerly a hospital. Today it's a cultural center with a wing dedicated to van Gogh that houses an art exhibit. *Info: place Dr. Félix Ray. Open daily. Admission: Free.*

place du Forum

There are many cafés at this attractive square, including **Café de la Nuit**. It's the one that looks like a vibrant van Gogh painting. Great people-watching here!

Fondation van Gogh

This van Gogh-themed gallery has no permanent collection. The gallery exhibits works of major contemporary artists paying homage to van Gogh in re-creations of his works. There is usually only one van Gogh painting here (or for that matter in all of Arles). The foundation is known for its contemporary architecture and design. You'll want to visit the rooftop terrace and check out the colored glass on the ceiling of the bookshop When van Gogh and fellow painter Paul Gauguin worked together in Arles in 1888, they were treated rather badly. This gallery seems to be an attempt to correct that wrong. *Info: 35 rue du Docteur Fanton. www.fondation-vincentvangogh-arles.org. Tel.*

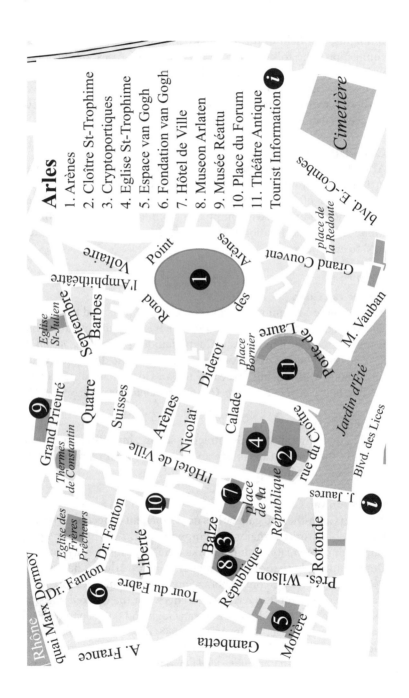

Arles

1. Arènes
2. Cloître St-Trophime
3. Cryptoportiques
4. Eglise St-Trophime
5. Espace van Gogh
6. Fondation van Gogh
7. Hôtel de Ville
8. Museon Arlaten
9. Musée Réattu
10. Place du Forum
11. Théâtre Antique
Tourist Information

04/90.93.08.08. Open daily 11am-7pm. Sometimes closed between exhibits. Admission: €9.

Musée Réattu

This art museum is named after Provençal artist Jacques Réattu. In addition to his works and some 16th-century tapestries, you'll find drawings, etchings and paintings by such notables as Picasso and Gauguin. *Info: rue du Grand Prieuré. Tel. 04/90.49.37.58. Open 10am-5pm (Oct-Mar until 6pm). Closed Mon. Admission: €8.*

place de la République

The main square in Arles (*photo below*). Take in the **Hôtel de Ville** (City Hall) dating back to the 1600s. The **obelisk** with its carved features is thought to have been a trophy from the conquest of Egypt by Rome during the reign of Emperor Augustus.

Eglise St-Trophime/Cloître St-Trophime

The vivid frieze of the Last Judgment in the doorway, a Roman sarcophagus and the cloisters are masterpieces of medieval architecture. The recently restored portal shows Christ with life-sized apostles in the columns below. *Info: place de la République. Open daily. Admission: Free. €6 to the cloister.*

Cryptoportiques

If your time is limited, skip this sight. No one is really certain of the purpose these ancient underground crypts served, which date back to 30 B.C. In World War II, they harbored the French Resistance. *Info: rue Balze. Tel. 04/90.49.36.74. Open daily 9am-noon and 2pm-6pm. Admission: €4.*

Musée de l'Arles Antique (Museum of Ancient Arles)

This modern, blue, triangular museum is located on the site of a huge Roman chariot-racing *cirque* (stadium). Mosaics, sculptures and detailed models of ancient monuments as they existed are all on view here. Most come to see the world's most famous collection of carved sarcophagi. *Info: presqu'île du Cirque Romain (1/2 mile south of the center city). Tel. 04/13.31.51.03. Open Wed-Mon 10am to 6pm. Closed Tue. Admission: €8.*

Théâtre Antique

Arles has two important Roman ruins. This ancient theatre is used today as a stage for festivals. It was built in the 1st century B.C. and seated 20,000. All that remains now are two columns. You can pretty much see all of it by looking over the fence from rue du Cloître. *Info: rue de la Calade. Tel. 04.90.49.36.74. Open daily May-Sep 9am-7pm, Mar, Apr and Oct 9am-6pm, Nov-Feb 10am-5pm. Admission: €6.50.*

Arènes

The highlight of your trip to Arles will likely be a visit to one of the most spectacular Roman monuments in Provence (*see photo on page 150*). The well-preserved arena with its two tiers of arches and four medieval towers once held over 20,000 spectators. It still hosts bullfights. Some are the traditional gory type and others are "Provence style" where the bull isn't killed. *Info: Rond Point des Arènes. www.*

arenes-arles.com. Tel. 04.90.49.36.36. Open daily May-Sep 9am-7pm, Mar, Apr and Oct 9am-6pm, Nov-Feb 10am-5pm. Admission: €6.50.

Abbaye de Montmajour

The ruins of this massive Romanesque abbey sit in the middle of marshland north of Arles. You can visit the now vacant abbey and its peaceful cloister. Van Gogh came here often to paint. *Info: Three miles (five km) northeast of Arles on route D17. Tel. 04/90.54.64.17. Open daily Apr-Jun 9:30am-6pm, Jul-Sep 10am-6:30pm, Oct-Mar 10am-5pm. Closed Mon Oct-Mar. Admission: €7.50.*

Les Alyscamps

If you have time, you can squeeze in a visit to one of the world's most famous cemeteries, to see Greek, Roman and Christian tombs. *Info: rue Pierre-Renaudel/avenue des Alyscamps (1/2 mile southeast from the city center). Tel. 04/90.49.36.74. Open daily 10am-noon and 2pm-5pm (until 6pm in the summer). Admission: €4.*

BEST SLEEPS & EATS

Nord-Pinus €€-€€€

This famous hotel has 27 rooms and an equally famous restaurant. It's centrally located in historic Arles on the place du Forum. Antiques

fill the common areas, and the rooms are interestingly decorated and well-maintained. The hotel is decorated with old bullfighting posters (many bullfighters have stayed here), interesting black-and-white photographs of Africa by Peter Beard, and mosaics. *Info: place du Forum. www.nord-pinus.com. Tel. 04/90.93.44.44. V, MC, AE. Restaurant, bar, AC, TV, telephone, WiFi.*

Hôtel Calendal €€

This is a favorite in Arles. Located near the arena, most of its 38 basic rooms (shower in bathroom, no bathtub) are on a shaded courtyard. Rooms vary in size, so ask to see before you commit. Smaller rooms are much cheaper. Kid-friendly. *Info: 5 rue Porte de Laure. Tel.*

04/90.96.11.89. www.lecalendal.com. V, MC, DC, AE. AC, TV, hairdryer, WiFi.

Hôtel de l'Amphithéâtre €
This hotel in a beautifully restored ancient building is located in the heart of the Old Town near the arena and the ancient theater. A great location for touring the main sights of Arles. Stone steps lead up to the adequate guest rooms. *Info: 5-7 rue Diderot. www.hotelamphitheatre.fr. Tel. 04/90.96.10.30. V, MC, AE. AC, TV, telephone.*

Brasserie Nord-Pinus €€-€€€
Wonderful and innovative French and Provençal cuisine, excellent service and beautiful surroundings (including an ancient Roman column) make this hotel restaurant a great dining experience. There's terrace dining in warm weather and a great bar (the Corrida). *Info: place du Forum. Tel. 04/90.93.44.44. Closed Sun and Mon.*

La Gueule du Loup €€
French and Provençal specialties are served in this small and comfortable restaurant. It's located in a stone building near the arena. You enter the restaurant through the kitchen. Try the *caillette d'agneau* (lamb baked in Provençal herbs). *Info: 39 rue des Arènes. Tel. 04/90.96.96.69. Closed Sun and Mon.*

Bistrot à Vins €€
You can either sit at the counter or at one of the small tables at this friendly wine bar. Excellent selection of Provençal wines by the glass. You can pair your wine with a delicious *tartes* or from a selection of straight-forward local dishes. *Info: 2 rue Dr. Fanton. Tel. 04/90.52.00.65. Closed Mon and Tue.*

L'Atelier Jean-Luc Rabanel €€€
Modern Provençal cuisine is featured at this award-winning restaurant. There is no written menu as dishes change based upon what is available from local sources. The restaurant is known for its large wine list. You'll find Asian influences in the chef's innovative dishes. Lunch begins at €60 and dinner begins at €110. **Bistro Acote** is a few doors down and is overseen by Chef Rabanel. It serves a fixed-price menu for €30. *Info: 7 rue des Carmes. www.rabanel.com. Tel.*

04/90.91.07.69. Closed Mon and Tue. Reservations required. Bistro Acote: www.bistro-acote.com. Tel. 04/90.47.61.13.

For those who want luxury accommodations and to dine at the restaurant, there are room and dining packages that begin at €250. There's also a cooking school. *Reservations through www.rabanel.com. Classes from €145.*

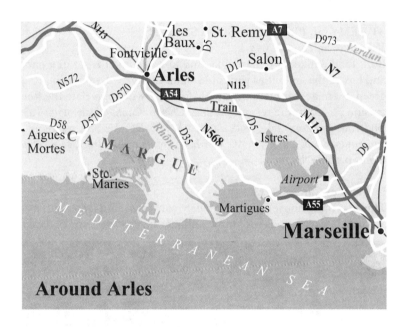

Around Arles

ST-RÉMY-DE-PROVENCE

Let's unwind in sophisticated **St-Rémy-de-Provence**. It's 12 miles (19 km) south of Avignon/15 miles (24 km) northeast of Arles. St-Rémy-de-Provence can be reached from Avignon by bus (45 minutes).

Nostradamus, credited with predicting much of the modern era, was born here in 1503. But even he couldn't have foreseen that 500 years later so many would find this the perfect Provence town. Roman ruins are within walking distance of the mansions that grace its historic center. Its most famous resident was Vincent van Gogh, and you can visit the asylum where he spent the last year of his life. But St-Rémy isn't about madness, it's about a calm and sophisticated town where you can experience the best of Provençal life. Boulevards Gambetta, Mirabeau, Marceau and Victor Hugo circle the town and are lined with cafés and boutiques. Take time to wander the maze of streets in the **Vieille Ville** (Old Town).

The large church **Collégiale St-Martin** was rebuilt in 1820 (the original church collapsed). Frequent concerts are held featuring its 5000-pipe organ. *Info: boulevard Marceau. Open daily. Admission: Free.*

ST-RÉMY-DE-PROVENCE SLEEPS & EATS
Vallon de Valrugues €€€
Built to look like an Italian villa, this 50-room hotel is set in a park and has all the amenities you could want. Golfers will love its putting green, there are tennis courts, and "foodies" will appreciate the fine cuisine served in the restaurant. *Info: Chemin Canto-Cigalo. www.vallondevalrugues.com. Tel. 04/90.92.04.40. V, MC, DC, AE. Spa, restaurant, bar, outdoor pool, gym, TV, AC, telephone, minibar, hairdryer, safe, Wifi. Closed part of Feb.*

Le Mas des Carassins €€
This *mas* (farmhouse) has been nicely converted into a 14-room hotel complete with pool, restaurant and mature gardens. *Info: 1 Chemin*

Gaulois. www.masdescarassins.com. Tel. 04/90.92.15.48. V, MC, AE. Restaurant, outdoor pool, cable TV, minibar, WiFi.

Sous les Figuiers €-€€
Just a five-minute walk from town, this interesting 14-room boutique hotel is popular with artists. The owner offers painting classes (beginning at €85). You can relax or paint in the lovely garden under the fig trees. *Info: 3 ave. Gabriel St-Réne Taillandier. www. hotel-charme-provence.com. Tel. 04/32.60.15.40. V, MC. AC, telephone, safe, WiFi.*

Hôtel du Soleil €
Just a short walk from the center of town, this hotel is surrounded by gardens, has an outdoor pool, and is decorated in a Provençal theme. Rooms have small, tiled bathrooms. *Info: 35 ave. Pasteur. Tel. 04/90.92.00.63. www.hotelsoleil.com. V, MC, DC, AE. Spa, bar, outdoor pool, TV, AC, telephone, hairdryer, safe. Closed Nov-Feb.*

Les Terrasses de l'Image €€€
Located in the Hôtel de l'Image (€€-€€€), in what once was the town's first hotel. Contemporary Provençal cuisine. Try the *poulet fermier* (free-range chicken) served in a citrus sauce. This is a lovely place to have a leisurely lunch for €30. *Info: 36 blvd. Victor Hugo. www.hotel-image.fr. Tel. 04/90.92.51.50. Open daily.*

The cocktail bar here is located in a former movie theater. A great place to end your evening even if you're not dining at the restaurant.

Bistrot Découverte €€
This wine bar and bistro is located in the center of St-Rémy. It's known for its list of Provençal wines from small producers. When dining here, try the delicious *la sourie d'agneau de 4 heures, jus à l'ait et au thym* (lamb shank cooked for four hours with a garlic and herb sauce). *Info: 19 blvd. Victor Hugo. www.bistrotdecouverte.com.Tel. 04/90.92.34.39. Closed Oct to mid-Mar.*

SHOPPING
Portes Anciennes
Fascinating collection of antique doors. Located on the outskirts of town (on the route d'Avignon). *Info: route d'Avignon. www.portesanciennes.com. Tel. 04/90.92.13.13. Open Mon-Sat 8:30am-noon and 2pm-6pm.*

There are several other antiques stores nearby.

A popular and colorful **market** is held Wednesday mornings in and around the place de la République. Great place to find Provençal olive oil.

Joel Durand
Calling all chocoholics! Sample some of the best chocolates in Provence at this small shop. The specialty here is a chocolate with

lavender! *Info: 7 boulevard Victor Hugo. Tel. 04/90.92.38.25. Closed Sun and Mon.*

GLANUM

The ancient town of **Glanum** is located on route D5 in the direction of Les Baux (1/2 mile [1 km] south of St-Rémy).

The ruins here date back to the 2nd century B.C. You can stroll the streets and building foundations and visit the **Arc Municipal** (arch) from the time of Julius Caesar. Across the street you'll find **Les Antiques,** two incredibly well-preserved monuments: the Arc Triomphal (dating from A.D. 20) and the **Mausolée** (a mausoleum dating from 30 B.C.). *Info: On D5 in the direction of Les Baux (1/2 mile [1 km] south of St-Rémy). Tel. 04/90.92.23.79. Open Apr-Sep 9:30am-6:30pm, Oct-Mar 10am-5pm. Closed Mon Sep-Mar. Admission: €7.50.*

The **Monastère de St-Paul-de-Mausole** is near Glanum off of route D5 in the direction of Les Baux.

This isolated asylum, a former monastery, still welcomes those in need of help. Its most famous patient, **Vincent van Gogh**, came here to spend the last year of his life after he allegedly cut off part of his left ear. During his stay, he painted such works as *Olive Trees*. You can tour the columned cloister (with a beautiful garden in the center) and the Romanesque chapel. *Info: avenue Edgar-le-Roy (near Glanum off D5 in the direction of Les Baux). Tel. 04/90.92.77.00. Open daily 9:30am-6:30pm Apr-Sep, 10:15am-4:30pm Mar. Closed Jan and Feb. Admission: €5.*

LES BAUX-DE-PROVENCE

Perched on limestone, **Les Baux-de-Provence** is one of the most dramatic and majestic sights in Provence. It's 11 miles (18 km) northeast of Arles/18 miles (29 km) south of Avignon. Le Baux can be reached from Avignon by bus (65 minutes).

It's hard to distinguish between the buildings and the rocks. The medieval town was home to one of the finest courts in medieval Provence. Abandoned in the 17th century, today it's one of the most visited sights in France.

Les Baux gets its name from the mineral bauxite (used in the production of aluminum), which was discovered in the neighboring hills. The village is filled with galleries, boutiques and cafés operating from the stone houses. On rue Frédéric-Mistral is the Renaissance **Hôtel de Manville**. It's the **Mairie** (Town Hall), and you can visit its courtyard and see changing exhibits. At place St-Vincent you can take in the view, or visit the church **Eglise St-Vincent**, a museum housing works of local artist Yves Brayer, and the small **Chapelle des Pénitents** for a short concert of ancient music.

The main cobbled street is an uphill 15-minute walk. It's hard to describe the clifftop. As you walk among the ruins, you feel like you're in another world. Come here to experience a breathtaking sunset. The famous **L'Oustau de la Baumanière**, a luxury hotel complex that has been a favorite of everyone from Picasso to Elizabeth Taylor, is also here.

The walls of the ruined citadel of **Château des Baux** date from the 10th century when the first lords settled on this limestone crag. The area below is called the **Val d'Enfer** (Valley of Hell). The **Tour du Brau** still guards the entrance and houses the **Musée d'Histoire des Baux**, filled with models of the town over the ages, medieval weapons, and relics. In the small **Chapelle St-Blaise** you can watch a 10-minute film featuring olive orchards painted by van Gogh, Gauguin and Cézanne. Excellent English audioguide. On weekends from April through September, the castle presents medieval pageants. *Info: www.chateaubaux-provence.com. Tel. 04/90.54.55.56. Open daily Apr-Jun and Sep 9am-7:15pm, Jul and Aug 9am-8:15pm, Jan-Feb and Nov-Dec 10am-5pm, Mar and Oct 9:30am-6:30pm. Admission: €10.*

Carrière des Lumières

You can watch a state-of-the-art, 40-minute slide show in a former quarry, where 50 projectors flash images on the limestone walls. It's mesmerizing. There is a new program each year. *Info: Val d'Enfer (Valley of Hell). Below Les Baux on route D27. www.carrieres-lumieres. com. Tel. 04/90.54.38.65. Open daily 10am-6pm Oct-Dec and Mar. Open 9:30am-7pm Apr-Sep. Closed Jan and Feb. Admission: €10.50.*

LES-BAUX-DE-PROVENCE SLEEPS & EATS

Auberge de la Benvengudo €€-€€€

A country house that's been lovingly converted to a charming hotel one mile south of Les Baux. Surrounded by gardens, the rooms and apartments are each beautifully decorated with antique furniture. All rooms have either a patio or balcony. The smaller rooms are a good deal. Beautiful outdoor pool. *Info: Vallon de l'Arcoule (on D78, the route to Arles). www.benvengudo.com. Tel. 04/90.54.32.54. V, MC, AE. Restaurant, outdoor pool, tennis courts, AC, TV, telephone, WiFi. Closed Nov-Feb.*

La Riboto de Taven €€-€€€

This 1835 farmhouse, outside of town in the "Valley of Hell," has been converted to an inn. The family-run restaurant and inn is known for its innovative cooking. There are six tastefully decorated rooms and apartments (located in grottos). Great outdoor pool and lovely gardens. *Info: Le Val d'Enfer (specific directions are given when you make reservations). www.taven-residences.fr. Tel. 04/90.54.34.23. V, MC, AE.*

Restaurant, outdoor pool, tennis court. AC, TV, telephone, minibar, WiFi. Closed Jan and Feb.

La Reine Jeanne €

This small inn, located at the entrance to the village, has an attractive terrace and restaurant. There are 10 basic and clean rooms. Bathrooms have shower stalls only. *Info: grande rue Baux. www.la-reinejeanne. com. Tel. 04/90.54.32.06. V, MC. Restaurant, bar, AC, TV. Closed Jan 15-31.*

Auberge de la Benvengudo €€€

Authentic Provençal cuisine, such as *gigot d'Agneau aux pigons* (leg of lamb with pine nuts) served at this lovely country house and inn located one mile south of Les Baux. There's an impressive list of regional wines. Fixed three-course menu only. *Info: Vallon de l'Arcoule (on D78, the route to Arles). www.benvengudo.com. Tel. 04/90.54.32.54. Reservations required. Closed Tue in winter.*

Le Café des Baux €€€

You'll find Provençal cooking and a fine wine list at this restaurant located steps from the entrance to the castle. The restaurant is known for its desserts, so save room for the delicious and interesting *crème brûlée à la lavande* (lavender *crème brûlée*). *Info: rue du Trencat. www. cafedesbaux.com. Tel. 04/90.54.52.69. Closed mid-Nov to mid-Mar. Also closed one day a week, but that day varies.*

THE CAMARGUE

The **Camargue** – the land of French cowboys – is 9 miles (15 km) south of Arles on route D570/12 miles (19 km) east of Aigues-Mortes.

This huge (309 square miles) area is a wetlands delta where the Rhône River breaks in two before spilling into the Mediterranean Sea. It's mostly swamp, and mosquitoes are bothersome. The only people who seem to be able to tolerate the conditions are *gardiens*, cowboys who ride white horses and raise bulls here. Part of The Camargue is filled with rice fields, cattle ranches and stud farms. The other part is **Parc Regional de Camargue** (a national park). It's home to thousands of flamingos, and is a bird-lovers paradise. The **Parc Ornithologique du Pont de Gau** is a protected area for over 400 species of birds. You can spend an entire day here exploring this national park, away from all the other tourists.

STES-MARIES-DE-LA-MER

Stes-Maries-de-la-Mer is 24 miles (39 km) south of Arles/10 miles (18 km) south of the Camargue/80 miles (129 km) west of Marseille.

According to legend, Mary Magdalene, Mary Salome and Mary Ja-cobé left ancient Israel and landed in a boat here. Depending on which version you believe, they either arrived with, or were greeted and helped by, Sara, a gypsy. The town, which has a whitewashed Spanish flavor to it, is a budget beach resort and very touristy. In May and October, it's loaded with gypsies who come to the town's church as part of a pilgrimage to honor Sara.

You can't miss the church **Eglise des Stes-Maries** with its large bell tower. The dark interior is filled with notes of thanks to the three Saint Marys. Note the carved boat with statues of Mary Magdalene and the Virgin Mary. The observation area has views of the town, its beaches and the Camargue. *Info: Open daily. Admission: Free. €2 (to observation area).*

There are plenty of casual and inexpensive eateries. There are also many places to ride the famous white horses that are raised here on route D570 as you enter town.

AIGUES-MORTES

Not too far from Stes-Maries-de-la-Mer is another touristy, but peculiar, town. **Aigues-Mortes** is 11 miles (19 km) northwest of Stes-Maries-de-la-Mer/29 miles (48 km) southwest of Arles/ /25 miles (41 km) south of Nîmes.

France's best-preserved walled town, Aigues-Mortes means "dead waters," an appropriate name, as it's surrounded by swamp. It was once a port town and departure point for Louis IX and his crusaders bound for the Holy Land. Inside the fortress walls is a small village.

Among the many souvenir shops is the stark church **Eglise Notre-Dame des Sablons** and the attractive **place St-Louis** dominated by a statue of Louis IX (*see photo below*). The **Tour de Constance** is a tower (complete with elevator) that affords views of The Camargue for €6.

11. Marseille

HIGHLIGHTS
• The Old Port and seafood restaurants in Marseille

• Sunbathing on the beach in Cassis and Bandol

• The fjord-like Calanques

• Les Gorges du Verdon

INTRO
Cosmopolitan and diverse **Marseille**, the breathtaking **Grand Canyon du Verdun**, vineyards and seafront resorts offer the traveler a little bit of everything in this area of Provence.

Marseille was founded over 2,600 years ago, making it France's oldest city. It's also the second largest city in France. Many travelers, put off by its urban sprawl, avoid it, as most come to this part of the country for quiet villages. Those who do choose to spend time here will be rewarded, as Marseille is a vibrant, exotic (check out one of the many **Arab markets**) and cosmopolitan city. Marseille was designated the European Capital of Culture for 2013. As a result, new museums have opened, older museums have been renovated, and many neighborhoods have been transformed.

COORDINATES

Marseille (population 850,000) is in the south of France on the Mediterranean Sea. It's 411 miles (662km) south of Paris and 117 miles (188km) west of Nice.

The **Marseille Airport** (located in Marignane) is 17 miles northwest of the city. Minivans (called *navettes*) leave for Marseille's St-Charles rail station every 20 minutes for €9. Bus and Métro tickets are €1.70 single ride, €5 day, 3 days for €10.50.

SIGHTS

Vieux Port (Old Port)

Industrial shipping has moved away from the Old Port, and now mostly pleasure boats are docked here. If arriving by car, follow the signs to Centre-Ville and Vieux Port. From the train station, Gare St-Charles, it's a 15-minute downhill walk to the port. It's dominated by two forts (**Fort St-Jean** – *photo on previous page* – and **Fort St-Nicolas**), and is still the heart of the city. You'll find a huge fish market here every day until early afternoon.

On the port is the ornate **Hôtel de Ville** (City Hall). If you walk uphill from City Hall, you'll be in **Le Panier** (Old Town), the oldest section of Marseille. Wander the tiny squares, cobblestone streets and stone stairways. Thankfully, after years of neglect, the Old Town is coming back to life.

At the top of Le Panier is the **Centre de la Vieille Charité** (Center of the Old Charity). This spectacular 17th-century building (a former poorhouse) houses two museums: the **Musée d'Arts Africains, Océaniens, et Amérindiens** (Museum of African, Oceanic and American Indian Art) and the **Musée d'Archéologie Mediterranéenne** (Museum of Mediterranean Archeology). *Info: 2 rue de la Charité (at the top of the Old Town). Tel.*

BOUILLABAISSE

Don't leave Marseille without trying its world-renowned *bouillabaisse*. There are two main varieties: *bouillabaisse du pêcheur* (with three types of fish) and *bouillabaisse du ravi* (with six different types of fish). Delicious! One great place known for this specialty is Miramar on the Old Port at 12 quai du port. €€€

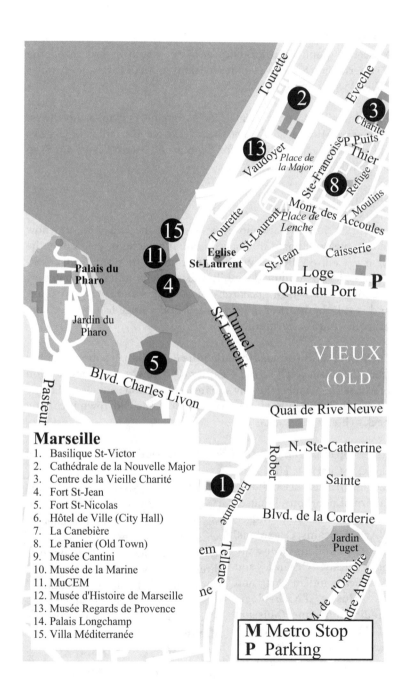

Tourette

Eveche

Charite

Vaudoyer

Ste-Francoise

P Puits

Thier

Place de la Major

Refuge

Mont des Accoules

Moulins

Place de Lenche

Tourette

St-Laurent

St-Jean

Caisserie

Eglise St-Laurent

Loge

Quai du Port

P

Palais du Pharo

Jardin du Pharo

Tunnel St-Laurent

VIEUX (OLD

Blvd. Charles Livon

Pasteur

Quai de Rive Neuve

N. Ste-Catherine

Rober

Sainte

Marseille

1. Basilique St-Victor
2. Cathédrale de la Nouvelle Major
3. Centre de la Vieille Charité
4. Fort St-Jean
5. Fort St-Nicolas
6. Hôtel de Ville (City Hall)
7. La Canebière
8. Le Panier (Old Town)
9. Musée Cantini
10. Musée de la Marine
11. MuCEM
12. Musée d'Histoire de Marseille
13. Musée Regards de Provence
14. Palais Longchamp
15. Villa Méditerranée

Endoume

Blvd. de la Corderie

Jardin Puget

em

Tellene

M. de l'Oratoire

ne

ndre Aune

M Metro Stop
P Parking

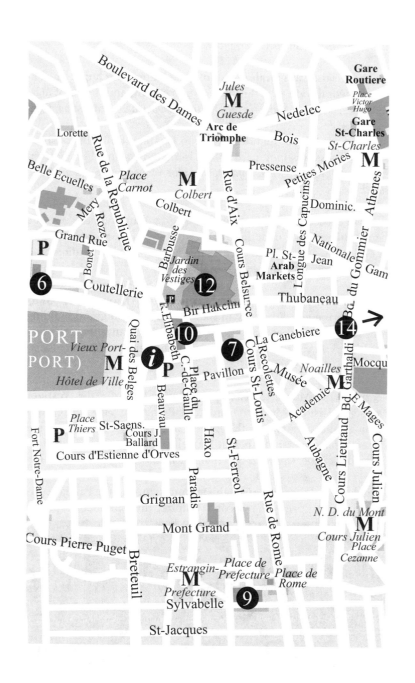

Boulevard des Dames

Lorette

Jules
M
Guesde

Nedelec

**Gare
Routiere**

*Place
Victor
Hugo*

**Arc de
Triomphe**

Bois

**Gare
St-Charles**
St-Charles

Pressense

Petites Mories

M

Belle Ecuelles

Rue de la Republique

*Place
Carnot*

M
Colbert

Colbert

Rue d'Aix

Dominic.

Athenes

Mery

Roze

Grand Rue

Bonet

Barbusse

*Jardin
des
Vestiges*

Cours Belsunce

Longue des Capucins

Pl. St-
**Arab
Markets**
Jean

Nationale

Gam

Bd. du Gommier

P

6

Coutellerie

R.Elizabeth

P

Bir Hakcim

Thubaneau

P
ORT
PORT)

Vieux Port-

M

Hôtel de Ville

Quai des Belges

i
P

10

Place du
C.-de-Gaulle

7

Pavillon

La Canebiere

Cours St-Louis

Cours St-Louis

Musée

Noailles

M

Mocqu

14

E Mages

Cours Julien

*Place
Thiers*
P

St-Saens.

Cours J.
Ballard

Beauvau

Haxo

St-Ferreol

Academie

Aubagne

Cours Lieutaud

Bd. Garibaldi

Fort Notre-Dame

Cours d'Estienne d'Orves

Grignan

Paradis

Mont Grand

Rue de Rome

N. D. du Mont
M
Cours Julien
*Place
Cezanne*

Cours Pierre Puget

Breteuil

Estrangin-
M
Prefecture
Sylvabelle

*Place de
Prefecture*

*Place de
Rome*

9

St-Jacques

04/91.14.58.80. Open Tue-Sun 10am-6pm. Closed Mon. Admission: €3 for each museum. No English information.

Also here is the **Cathédrale de la Nouvelle Major.** This huge 19th-century cathedral, located in the Old Town, is neo-Byzantine (lots of marble). *Info: place de la Major (in the Old Town). Open daily. Admission: Free.*

Ferries depart from quai des Belges to **Château d'If.** This offshore island fortress was long used as a prison, and was made famous in the *Count of Monte Cristo. Info: Open daily. Admission: €6. Ferry ride to island: €11.*

If you're interested in shopping, head to **La Canebière.** Marseille's main boulevard begins at the Old Port and stretches through the center of the city, and it's loaded with cafés, shops of all sorts, sailors, and people of every imaginable nationality.

At number 7 is the **Musée de la Marine et de L'Economie de Marseille** (Marine and Economy Museum), located in a grand building housing the Chamber of Commerce. Exhibits feature the city's marine history. *Info: 7 La Canebière. Tel. 04/91.39.33.21. Open Tue-Sun 10am-6pm. Closed Mon. Admission: €2.*

Nearby is the **Musée d'Histoire de Marseille/Jardin des Vestiges** (Marseille History Museum/Garden of Remains). View current archeological excavations in the garden, and visit the museum to see archeological finds from ancient Marseille. *Info: 2 rue Henri-Barbusse. Tel. 04/91.55.36.00. Open Tue-Sun 10am-6pm. Closed Mon. Admission: €5.*

If you keep walking up La Canebière, you'll run into the **Palais Longchamp.** Built during the Second Empire, this spectacular palace

won't disappoint with fountains, sculptures and columns. Both the fine-arts and natural-history museums are located here. *Info: place Bernex. Tel. 04/91.14.59.30. Open Tue-Sun 10am-6pm. Closed Mon. Admission: €5.*

On the other side of the Old Port from La Panier (Old Town) are two other sights you can see if you have the time. The basilica **Basilique St-Victor** sits above a 5th-century crypt said to contain the remains of the martyr St. Cassianus. *Info: place St-Victor. Tel. 04/96.11.22.60. Open daily 9am-7pm. Admission: Free. €2 to the crypt.*

The **Musée Cantini** is a modern-art museum featuring exhibits of some of the world's up-and-coming artists. The museum's permanent collection has a large collection of Surrealist art. Some of the artists featured here are Kandinsky, Dubuffet, Bacon, Signac, Léger, and Ernst. *Info: 19 rue Grignan. Tel. 04/91.54.77.75. Open Tue-Sun 10am-6pm. Closed Mon. Admission: €5.*

Notre-Dame de la Garde is topped by a gold statue of the Virgin Mary. This gigantic Romanesque-Byzantine basilica is 500 feet above the harbor. The elegant interior is filled with marble and mosaics, and the views outside are spectacular. *Info: rue Fort-du-Sanctuaire (30-minute walk from harbor). Open daily 7am-7pm. Admission: Free.*

Marseille has several new museums located near Fort-St-Jean in the Old Port.

Opened in 2013, **MuCEM** (Musée des Civilisations de L'Europe et de la Méditerranée – the Museum of European and Mediterranean Civilizations) houses a collection of 250,000 art and artifacts from areas around the Mediterranean. The contemporary building is encased in an interesting concrete "lace" and connected to the Fort St-Jean by a spectacular elevated walkway. *Info: Quai du Port. www.mucem.org. Tel. 04/96.13.80.90. Open Wed-Mon 11am-7pm in summer (until 6pm in winter). Late opening on Fridays until 10pm (May 2 - October 31). Closed Tue. Admission: Permanent and temporary exhibitions €8 (permanent exhibits only €5).*

For award-winning Mediterranean dining, **La Table du Môle** is located on the top of MuCEM (€€€). Fantastic views of the sea and port.

At lunch, you can dine at La Cuisine in the connected dining room (without the views). *Info: €€. Reservations through www.passedat.fr.*

Villa Méditerranée, next to MuCEM, host exhibits, performances, and concerts all with the theme of bringing together Mediterranean cultures. The modern building features a huge cantilevered overhang above a reflecting pool. The entire basement is below sea level. *Info: Esplanade de J4. www.villa-mediterranee.org Tel. 04/95.09.42.52. Open Tue-Thu noon-7pm, Fri noon-10pm, Sat and Sun10am-7pm. Closed Mon. Admission: €7.*

Located near MuCEM and Villa Méditerranée, the new **Musée Regards de Provence** features Provençal and Mediterranean art and media from the 18th to the 21st centuries. The real attraction here is the **rooftop restaurant** with incredible views of the nearby Cathédrale de la Nouvelle Major. It's hard to believe that this building was once the station where immigrants were disinfected prior to entry to France. *Info: Ave. Voudoyer. www.museeregardsdeprovence.com. Tel. 04/96.17.40.40. Open daily 10am-6pm. Admission: €6.*

MARKETS
Marseille has a large Tunisian, Algerian, and Moroccan population. You'll feel as if you are in North Africa at one of the city's large **Arab Markets**. The largest is found off of La Canebière on rue Longue des Capucins. Don't miss it!

There's a huge **fish market** at the Old Port on quai des Belges every day until early afternoon.

BEST SLEEPS & EATS
Sofitel Marseille (Vieux Port) €€€
This 133-room contemporary hotel above the old port offers modern conveniences and is popular with business travelers. Good location for seeing the port's major sights. *Info: 36 blvd. Charles-Livon. Tel. 04/91.15.59.00. www.sofitel.com. V, MC, DC, AE. Restaurant, bar, AC, TV, telephone, minibar, in-room safe, hairdryer, WiFi.*

The 110-room **Novotel (Vieux Port)** is in the same building, and shares some staff. This less expensive (€€) cousin has smaller rooms and fewer amenities, but is still a good choice. *Info: 36 blvd. Charles-*

Livon. www.novotel.com. Tel. 04/96.11.42.11. V, MC, DC, AE. Restaurant, bar, AC, TV, telephone, minibar, hairdryer, WiFi.

Les Arcenaulx €€-€€€
Provençal cuisine with outdoor dining near the Old Port. You can visit the connected bookstore after your meal. *Info: 25 cours d'Estienne d'Orves. www.les-arcenaulx.com. Tel. 04/91.59.80.30. Closed Sun.*

Chez Ida €€
Packed, popular, and fun. This restaurant is centrally located near place Jean Jaurès. Try the baked sea bass and the gazpacho. Strangely, it is a karaoke place some evenings. *Info: 7 rue Ferdinand Rey. www.chezida.fr. Tel. 04/91.47.04.97. Lunch Mon-Fri. Dinner Fri and Sat. Closed Sun.*

Bar de la Marine €€
On the Old Port, this bar is popular with locals for lunch. *Info: 15 quai de Rive-Neuve. Tel. 04/91.54.95.42. Open daily.*

Le Crystal €€
1950s-style lounge (complete with a collection of Formica wall clocks) with a view of the Old Port. If you're hungry, Le Crystal serves decent burgers, sandwiches, and salads. *Info: 148 quai du Port. www.lecrystal-vieuxport.com. Tel. 04/91.91.57.96. Open daily.*

BEST NIGHTLIFE & ENTERTAINMENT
Le Trollybus
Popular dance club featuring new wave, punk rock, techno, and retro music. *Info: 22 quai de Rive Neuve. Tel. 04/91.54.30.45.*

New Can Can
Not really so "new." This is Marseille's oldest gay disco. *Info: 22 rue Beauveau. www.newcancan.com. Tel. 04/91.33.79.20.*

La Caravelle
Jazz lovers can head to this bar, restaurant, and club located on the Old Port. *Info: 34 quai du Port. www.lacaravelle-marseille.com. Tel. 04/91.90.36.64.*

Opéra Municipal
Opera and classical-music concerts. *Info: 2 rue Molière. www.opera-marseille.fr. Tel. 04/91.55.11.10.*

CASSIS, BANDOL, & THE CALANQUES
The coast of Provence offers you the choice of two relaxing port towns. First, we'll head to **Cassis**. It's 19 miles (30 km) east of Marseille/25 miles (42 km) west of Toulon.

Waterfront cafés around a beautiful port, buildings painted in pastels, boutiques and the **Château de Cassis** (a medieval castle) all make this Provence's most attractive coastal town. The water is clean and clear, and the beaches, like many others on this coast, are pebbly rather than sandy. The 1,200-foot cliff above the *château* is **Cap Canaille**, Eu-

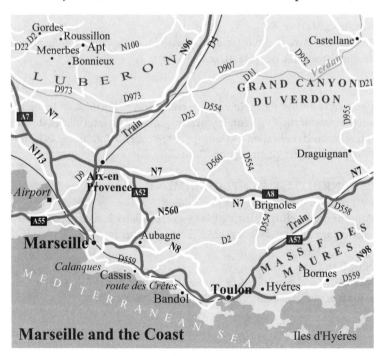

Marseille and the Coast

rope's highest coastal cliff. Frankly, there isn't much to do in Cassis except lie on the beach and either look at the castle or the beachgoers, but, after all, that's what you came here for. Parking is scarce in town, so you can park outside and take a shuttle bus into town (watch for the signs saying *navette*). They're free and depart every 15 minutes.

Don't forget to try the aromatic white wines that are produced in the hills surrounding Cassis. There are several vineyards outside of town that offer wine tastings. One is **Domaine Ferme Blanc**. *Info: on route D559, Tel. 04/42.01.00.74.*

Between Cassis and Bandol are the **Calanques**. Like fjords, these cliffs border the coast and hide beautiful beaches with clear blue water. You can either take a boat or hiking tour (several companies operate from the harbor in Cassis with tour prices beginning at €16) to explore the three *calanques*: **Calanque En Vau**, **Calanque Port Pin** and **Calanque Port Miou**. If you're not interested in hiking or the boat tour, the **route des Crêtes**, which heads east out of town following the signs for La Ciotat/Toulon, provides spectacular views of the coast. Note that this road is not for nervous drivers. It's very scary at points, with no guardrails protecting you from plunging straight down the cliff!

Bandol is 15 miles (24 km) southeast of Cassis/9 miles (15 km) west of Toulon. On the western end of the Côte d'Azur, this popular seaside resort town is best known for its beaches, seaside casino, yacht-filled harbor and waterfront promenade lined with palm trees. There are 25 hotels here, and even more eating establishments. Most know the town for the wine that carries its name. The red is full-bodied and spicy, while the white is fruity, often with a hint of aniseed.

CASSIS SLEEPS & EATS
Hôtel Mahogany €€-€€€
This 30-room hotel faces the Mediterranean and the coastal cliff. Nineteen of the rooms have balconies with sea views where you can

enjoy breakfast which is included in the price (and later a glass of Cassis wine). Great location for a short walk into town to dine or to the beach. The friendly staff is ready to help you with reservations for dinner or local activities. *Info: Plage du Bestouan. www.hotelmahogany. com. Tel. 04/42.01.05.70. V, MC. AC (in most rooms), TV, telephone, mini-bar, hairdryer. WiFi.*

During the summer, the hotel restaurant "**La Calanque M**" is open every evening and Sunday for lunch (€€€). The emphasis is on seafood, but you can also try the delicious *côte de veau au citron* (veal chop served in a citrus sauce).

Hôtel Royal Cottage €€
This 25-room hotel is located on the hillside only a five-minute walk to the port (it's a steep walk back). Comfortable and clean rooms, helpful staff and a delightful outdoor swimming pool surrounded by

palm trees where you can have a light lunch in the summer. *Info: 6 ave. du 11 Novembre. www.royal-cottage.com. Tel. 04/42.01.33.34. V, MC. Outdoor pool, AC, TV, telephone, minibar, in-room safe, hairdryer, WiFi.*

Hôtel de France Maguy €-€€
Located a few blocks from the port, this 10-room hotel has small, clean rooms. The more expensive rooms have little patios or balconies. There is secure, private parking. *Info: Ave. du Revestel. www. www.hoteldefrancemaguy.com. Tel. 04/42.01.72.21. V, MC, AE. AC, TV, telephone, hairdryer, WiFi.*

Chez Nino €€-€€€
Grilled fish, *bouillabaisse* and sea urchins (the local specialty) are what to expect at this harborside restaurant. *Info: Quai Barthélémy (on the harbor). www.nino-cassis.com. Tel. 04/42.01.74.32. Closed Mon, Sun (dinner) and mid-Dec to mid-Feb.*

Le Chaudron €€-€€€
This bistro is located on one of the backstreets of Cassis and not too far the port. It's family-run and friendly. Provençal cuisine with an emphasis on fresh seafood. Whatever you eat, make sure you order one of the local Cassis wines available here! *Info: 4 rue Adolphe Thiers. Tel. 04/42.01.74.18. Closed Tue. Lunch only on weekends.*

MASSIF DES MAURES

The **Massif des Maures** is between route N98 (the coastal road) and route A8. North from route N98 is the mountainous route D14. Hope you like hairpin turns!

It's hard to believe that this hilly, thickly wooded and sparsely populated area is so close to the frenetic coastal resorts of the western Riviera. The Massif des Maures stretches from Hyères to Fréjus, and much of it's inaccessible. The hills are by no means huge, but the sudden drops in the winding roads and the views make this an interesting detour from the touristy coast. There's a footpath called the GR9 for experienced hikers. "GR" stands for Grandes Randonnées, national hiking trails. It follows the highest ridge of the Massif des Maures.

LES GORGES DU VERDON

The Grand Canyon of Verdon – **Les Gorges du Verdon** – can be vis-

ited by traveling along two cliffside roads stretching from Moustiers-Ste-Marie to Castellane. **La Corniche Sublime** (routes D19 to D71) is along the southern rim including **Pont de l'Artuby**, the highest bridge in Europe. **La route des Crêtes** (routes D952 and D23) follows the northern rim including **Point Sublime**, the viewpoint at the entrance to the canyon. From here, the adventurous GR4 trail leads you to the bottom of the canyon, which can be reached only by foot or raft.

Hello, Gorgeous! The green waters of the Verdun River have sliced through limestone and created one of the great natural sights of not only Provence, but of France and all of Europe. This canyon is 13 miles long and as deep as 2,300 feet. At points, it's only 26 feet wide. The huge area around the canyon is a nature-lover's smorgasbord of pristine lakes, trickling streams, alpine scenery and picture-postcard villages such as **Aiguines** and **Moustiers-Ste-Marie** (*see photo on next page*). A drive around the canyon can take up to three hours and even longer in the summer. You'll need to fill your tank before you get to the canyon. Expect hairpin turns, along with fantastic scenery. There are many areas to stop and walk or just take in the breathtaking vistas.

MOUSTIERS-STE-MARIE SLEEPS & EATS
La Bastide de Moustiers €€€
Remote and surrounded by lavender fields, this highly sought-after 13-room hotel is decorated with local pottery and antiques. You can relax (or dine) at the beautiful small outdoor pool. Excellent restaurant serving innovative local and international cuisine. (€€€). *Info: Chemin de Quinson. www.bastide-moustiers.com. Tel. 04/92.70.47.47.*

V, *MC, AE. Restaurant, bar, pool, AC, TV, telephone, minibar, hairdryer, WiFi. Closed Jan-Feb.*

Les Santons €€€

Located in a 12th-century house next to the church, this small restaurant serves hearty fare (especially game dishes) flavored with Provençal herbs. Try the interesting lavender ice cream. *Info: Place de l'Eglise in Moustiers-Ste-Marie. www.lessantons.com. Tel. 04/92.74.66.48. Closed Mon.*

12. Practical Matters

GETTING TO THE SOUTH OF FRANCE
Airports/Arrival

The **Nice-Côte d'Azur Airport** is located on a peninsula 20 minutes west of the central city of Nice. A taxi into town costs at least €35. Buses run at least every 30 minutes to the central city for less €6. Purchase the Aéro Ticket for buses 98 and 99. Bus 99 runs from the airport to the Nice's main train station in 30 minutes. Bus 98 runs along the promenade des Anglais around the Old Town. The buses operate between 6am and 11pm. Check with the helpful staff at the airport bus station in Terminal 1. Once in Nice, hop on a bus or tram to get around town (€1.50 single ride, 10 tickets for €10).

There are also airport express shuttles to Monaco (#110), Cannes (#210), and Antibes (#250). Each runs hourly from Terminal 1. Check out www.lignesdazur.com.

The **Marseille Airport** (located in Marignane) is 17 miles northwest of the city. Minivans (called navettes) leave for Marseille's St-Charles rail station every 20 minutes for €9. Bus and Métro tickets are €1.70 single ride, €5 day, 3 days for €10.50).

All major car-rental companies are represented at both airports.

You can also fly to Paris and then take a train south (see next page).

GETTING AROUND
Cars & Driving

Renting a car and driving is the best way to see the areas covered in this book. Note that **parking can be difficult in high season**. Driving within major cities (Nice, Marseille and Avignon) can be a headache. Gas is very expensive, but a mitigating factor is that the cars are smaller and more energy-efficient. You will either take a ticket when you get on the autoroute and pay (look for the signs that say *péage*) when you get off, or pay as you go.

In order of fastest to slowest, routes are as follows: A means **autoroute**, N means **national route**, and D means **departmental route**. Be prepared for narrow roads, high speeds and hairpin turns.

KILOMETERS-MILES
One kilometer = 0.62 miles. To convert miles to kilometers, multiply by 1.61. So, 1 mile = 1.61 kilometers.

Train & Bus Travel
SNCF is the rail system for France. **TGV** trains are fast-speed trains that travel at up to 220 mph. TGV trains departing from Paris's Charles-de-Gaulle Airport serve:

- Aix-en-Provence, 3 hours
- Arles, 4 hours
- Avignon, 2 hours and 40 minutes
- Cannes, 6 hours via Marseille
- Nîmes, 3 hours
- Marseille, 3 hours and 15 minutes
- Orange, 3 hours

Aix-en-Provence and Avignon have TGV stations on the edge of town. **From Paris to Nice takes 6 hours on the TGV**, as not all of the trip is high-speed. **Info: www.sncf.com.**

There's a **coastal rail line** that runs from Ventimiglia on the Italian border (Vintimille in French) to Marseille. There are trains that run nearly every hour on this line. Stops on this scenic train ride include: Menton, Cap-Martin, Monaco, Èze-sur-Mer (not to be confused with hilltop Èze), Beaulieu, St-Jean-Cap-Ferrat, Villefranche-sur-Mer, Nice, Antibes and Cannes. Local trains serve many Provence and Riviera towns. You must validate (*composter*) your ticket at a machine (watch locals do it) before you get on a SNCF train.

Regional bus service is good, but is limited on Sundays. Train service is in most cases faster, but bus service is generally cheaper.

FESTIVALS

January
- Monte Carlo Motor Rally (*Le Rallye*) in Monte Carlo

February
- Lemon Festival (*Fête du Citron*) in Menton

February-March (Easter)
- Carnival in Nice
- Easter Bullfighting Festival (*Féria Pascale*) in Arles
- Procession of the Dead Christ (*Procession du Christ Mort*), a religious procession, in Roquebrune-Cap Martin
- Procession of the Penitents (*Procession des Pénitents*), religious processions in Collioure and Arles

April
- The Spring Arts Festival (*Printemps des Arts*), featuring symphonic, opera and ballet performances, held April to mid-May in Monte Carlo
- The Monte Carlo Tennis Tournament, held April to mid-May in Monte Carlo
- Olympic Sailing Week, a sailing competition featuring 1,000 boats from over 50 nations, in Hyères

May
- *Festival des Musiques d'Aujour d'hui*, a musical festival featuring young artists, in Marseille
- Festival of the Move to Summer Grazing (*Fête de la Transhumance*), a sheep drive to upland summer pastures, in St-Rémy. The entire town is loaded with sheep and goats in mid- to late May
- Cowboy Festival (*La Fête des Gardians*), a festival celebrating the cowboys from the Camargue, in Arles
- Gypsies' Pilgrimage (*Le Pélerinage des Gitans*), a gathering of Gypsies as part of a religious pilgrimage, in Stes-Maries-de-la-Mer
- International Film Festival (*Festival International du Film*) in Cannes
- *Grand Prix de Monaco*, auto race in mid-May, in Monte Carlo

June
- *Festival de Marseille Méditerranée*, Mediterranean music festival in late June and early July, in Marseille
- Classical music festival (*Festival Aix en Musique*) in Aix-en-Provence

- *Fête de la Tarasque*, a festival celebrating the legend of Tarasque (a dragon-like beast) being subdued by Saint Martha, in Tarascon
- *Reconstitution Historique*, a festival honoring Nostradamus, in Salon-de-Provence

July
- Bastille Day, celebrating the fall of the Bastille Prison, on July 14. Celebrations throughout the region
- Fishermen's Festival (*La Fête des Pècheurs*) in early July in Cassis
- *Festival d'Aix*, classical street performance, in Aix-en-Provence
- Beach Volleyball World Series in Marseille
- Musical festival (*Nuits Musicales d'Uzès*), last two weeks of July, in Uzès
- Festival of dance, theatre and music (*Festival d'Avignon*), the last three weeks of July and the first week of August, in Avignon
- Opera and classical music fair (*Les Chorégies d'Orange*) in Orange
- Musical and theatrical events (*Festival Lacoste*) in Lacoste (July and August)
- Jazz Festival, end of July, in Aix-en-Provence
- Jazz Festival in Juan-les-Pins
- Jazz Festival in Nice
- Nikaia, international athletics event, in Nice
- *Pétanque* Championships, (also known as *boules*), in Marseille
- Nightime Bull Festival (*Nuit Taurine*), the French version of Pamplona's "Running of the Bulls," in mid-July in St-Rémy

August
- Wine Festival (*Fête de la Véraison*), first weekend, in Châteauneuf-du-Pape
- *Fêtes Daudet*, a folk festival, in Fontvieille
- *Féria de St-Rémy*, a bull festival (including bull fights with matadors on horseback), in St-Rémy

September
- Rice Harvest Festival (*Féria des Prémices du Riz*), a regional festival including bullfights, in Arles
- Festival of Olives (*Journée de l'Olivier*), festival of the olive, in late-September in Salon-de-Provence

October

- Gypsies' Pilgrimage (*Le Pélerinage des Gitans*), a gathering of Gypsies as part of a religious pilgrimage, in Stes-Maries-de-la-Mer
- String Quartet Festival (*Musique en Pays*) late October and early November, in Fayence

November

- Santons Festival (*Marché aux Santons*), craft festival featuring *santons* (terra-cotta figurines), in Tarascon

December

- Christmas Fair (*Foire de Noël*), Christmas gift and ornament fair, in Mougins
- Provence Christmas (*Noël Provençal*), traditional procession of shepherds followed by Midnight Mass on Christmas Eve, in Les Baux
- *Santons* Fair (*Foire aux Santons*), craft festival featuring *santons* (terra-cotta figurines), in Marseille
- New Year's Eve (*Fête de St-Sylvestre*), everyone heads outdoors to the old town centers to celebrate

HOLIDAYS

- New Year's: January 1
- Easter
- Ascension (40 days after Easter)
- Pentecost (seventh Sunday after Easter)
- May Day: May 1
- Victory in Europe: May 8
- Bastille Day: July 14
- Assumption of the Virgin Mary: August 15
- All Saints': November 1
- Armistice: November 11
- Christmas: December 25

BASIC INFORMATION

Banking & Changing Money

The **euro** (€) is the currency of France and most of Europe. Before you leave for France, it's a good idea to get some euros. It makes your arrival a lot easier. Call your credit-card company or bank before you leave to tell them that you'll be using your ATM or credit card outside the country. Many have automatic controls that can "freeze" your account if the computer program determines that there are charges outside your normal area.

ATMs (with fees, of course) are the easiest way to change money in France. You'll find them everywhere. You can still get traveler's checks, but why bother? Especially since many establishments will not take them for fear of counterfeit checks.

Business Hours

Many attractions and offices in Provence close at noon and reopen and hour or two later.

Climate & Weather

Expect hot and dry weather except for periods of heavy rain in spring. November, December and January can be quite cold and wet, with temperatures dipping to lows in the upper 30s. The average high temperature in July and August is 84 degrees. The Mistral wind blows 30 to 60 miles per hour about 100 days of the year in Provence. It begins above the Alps and Massif Central Mountains, gaining speed as it heads south toward the Mediterranean Sea. It's worst in the Rhône Valley. Le Mistral is followed by clear skies.

Consulates & Embassies
- **US Consulate, Nice:** *7 avenue Gustave V, Tel. 04/93.88.89.55*
- **US Consulate, Marseille:** *place Varian-Fry, Tel. 01/43.12.47.54*
- **Canadian Consulate, Nice:** *2 place Franklin, Tel. 04/93.92.93.22*

Electricity

The electrical current in France is **220 volts** as opposed to 110 volts found at home. Don't fry your electric razor, hairdryer or laptop. You'll need a converter and an adapter. Some laptops don't require a converter, but why are you bringing them on vacation anyway?

Emergencies & Safety

Don't wear a fanny pack; it's a sign that you're a tourist and an easy target (especially in crowded tourist areas). Avoid wearing expensive jewelry. Don't leave valuables in your car. **In case of an emergency, dial 17 for the police, 15 for an ambulance and 18 for the fire department.** Pharmacies can refer you to a doctor.

Insurance

Check with your health-care provider. Most policies don't cover you overseas. If that's the case, you may want to obtain medical insurance. Given the uncertainties in today's world, you may also want to purchase **trip-cancellation insurance**. Make sure that your policy covers sickness, disasters, bankruptcy and State Department travel restrictions and warnings. In other words, read the fine print! Info: www.insuremytrip.com for insurance coverage.

Internet Access

Cyber cafés seem to pop up everywhere (and go out of business quickly). You shouldn't have difficulty finding a place to e-mail home. Remember that French keyboards are different than those found in the U.S. and Canada. WiFi is now readily available at hotels and cafes. To access the Internet, the cheaper option is to use free WiFi. Don't incur huge charges by incurring data roaming charges. Your best bet is to turn off data roaming on your phone when you're not trying to access the Internet.

If you want to use your smartphone and not worry about data or voice charges, simply turn off both data and voice roaming or place your phone in "Airport Mode" and then turn on WiFi. When you use WiFi exclusively, you can stay connected and avoid unnecessary charges.

Language

Please, make the effort to speak a little French. It will get you a long way, even if all you can say is *Parlez-vous anglais?* (par-lay voo ahn-glay): Do you speak English? Gone are the days when the French were only interested in correcting your French. There's a list of helpful French phrases in this book.

Packing

Never pack prescription drugs, eyeglasses or valuables. Carry them on. Think black. It always works for men and women. Oh, and by the way, pack light. Don't ruin your trip by having to lug around huge suitcases. Before you leave home, make copies of your passport, airline tickets and confirmation of hotel reservations. You should also make a list of your credit-card numbers and the telephone numbers for your credit-card companies. If you lose any of them (or they're stolen), you can call someone at home and have them provide the information to you. You should also pack copies of these documents separate from the originals.

Passport Regulations

You'll need a **valid passport** to enter France. If you're staying more than 90 days, you must obtain a visa. Canadians don't need visas. Canadians can bring back C$750 each year if they have been gone for 7 days or more.

US citizens who have been away more than 48 hours can bring home $800 of merchandise duty-free every 30 days. *Info: go to help.cbp.gov.*.

Postal Services

Post offices – **PTT** – are found in nearly every town. You'll recognize them by their **yellow La Poste signs**. They're generally open weekdays from 8am-7pm and Saturdays from 8am until noon. Some post offices, especially those in smaller towns, close for an hour or two in the middle of the day.

Rest Rooms

There aren't a lot of public rest rooms. If you need to go, your best bet is to head (no pun intended) to the nearest café or *brasserie*. It's considered good manners to purchase something if you use the rest room. Don't be shocked to walk into a rest room and find two porcelain footprints and a hole in the floor. These old "Turkish toilets" still exist. Hope you have strong thighs!

Taxes

Hotel and restaurant prices are required by law to include taxes and service charges. **Value Added Tax** (VAT or **TVA** in France) is nearly 20% (higher on luxury goods). The VAT is included in the price of goods (except services such as restaurants). Foreigners are entitled to a refund and must fill out a refund form. When you make your purchase, you should ask for the form and instructions if you're purchasing €175 or more in one place and in one day (no combining). Yes, it can be a hassle. *Info: Check out www.globalrefund.com for the latest information on refunds (and help for a fee)*

Telephone
• Country code for France is **33**

- Area code for Provence and the French Riviera is 04
- Calls beginning with 0800 are toll-free
- Calling France from the U.S. and Canada: dial 011-33-4 plus the eight-digit local number. You drop the 0 in the area code
- Calling the U.S. or Canada from Paris: dial 00 (wait for the tone), dial 1 plus the area code and local number
- Calling within Provence and the French Riviera: dial 04 and the eight-digit local number.

Phone cards are the cheapest way to call. Get one from many *tabacs, métro* stations or magazine kiosks.

A great way to stay in touch and save money is to **rent an international cell phone**. One provider is *www.cellhire.com*. Some cell phones purchased in the U.S. do not work in Europe. If you're a frequent visitor to Europe, you may want to purchase a cell phone (for about $50) from *www.mobal.com*. You'll get an international telephone number, and pay for calls by the minute. Many smartphones work in Europe. Contact your provider to access a global plan for the time period you will be in Europe. When in Europe, minimize roaming charges by using WiFi. For more information on avoiding charges on your smartphone while in Europe, see the "Internet Access" section above.

Time
When it's noon in New York City, it's 6pm in Provence. For hours of events or schedules, the French use the 24-hour clock. So 6am is 06h00 and 1pm is 13h00.

Tipping
In **restaurants**, a service charge is almost always added to your bill. Depending on the service, it's sometimes appropriate to leave up to 5%. Most locals round up to the next euro and it's okay if that is what you do, too. Travelers from the U.S. sometimes have trouble not tipping. Remember, you do not have to tip. The menu will usually note that service is included (*service compris*). Sometimes this is abbreviated with the letters **s.c.** The letters **s.n.c.** stand for *service non compris*; this means that the service is not included in the price, and you must leave a tip. This is extremely rare. You'll sometimes find *couvert* (cover charge) on your menu, which is a small charge just for placing your butt at the table). **Other tips:** 10% for taxi drivers, €1 for room service,

€1.50 per bag to the hotel porter, €1.50 per day for maid service and €0.50 to bathroom attendants.

Tourist Information
Most towns in this book have helpful tourist-information centers. Tourist offices in Nice, Avignon, and Arles sell money-saving museum passes.

Water
Tap water is safe in France. Occasionally, you'll find *non potable* signs in rest rooms. This means that the water is not safe for drinking.

Web Sites
For the French Government Tourist Office go to *www.franceguide. com*. For the US State Department Foreign Entry Requirements go to *www.state.gov*.

HOTELS & RESTAURANTS
Hotel Prices in this Book
Prices for two people in a double room:
- **Expensive** (over €200): €€€
- **Moderate** (€100-200): €€
- **Inexpensive** (under €100): €

Restaurant Advice
Eat at a **neighborhood restaurant or bistro.** You'll always know the price of a meal before entering, as almost all restaurants post the menu and prices in the window. Never order anything whose price is not known in advance. If you see *selon grosseur* (sometimes abbreviated as **s/g**) this means that you're paying by weight, which can be extremely expensive.

Delis and **food stores** can provide cheap and wonderful meals. Buy some cheese, bread, wine and other snacks and have a picnic. In fact, no matter what, you should go into a *boulangerie* and buy a *baguette* at least once. Remember to pack a corkscrew and eating utensils when you leave home.

Lunch, even at the most expensive restaurants listed in this guide, always has a lower fixed price. So have lunch as your main meal. Many French do.

Restaurants and bistros that have menus written in English (especially those near tourist attractions) are almost always more expensive than neighborhood restaurants and bistros.

Street vendors in larger towns generally sell inexpensive and terrific food; you'll find excellent hot dogs, crêpes and roast-chicken sandwiches.

For the cost of a cup of coffee or a drink, you can linger at a café and watch the world pass you by for as long as you want. It's one of France's greatest bargains.

Restaurant prices in this book are for a main course and without wine:
• **Expensive:** (over €20) €€€
• **Moderate:** (€10-20) €€
• **Inexpensive:** (under €10) €

The bill in a restaurant is called *l'addition* ... but the bill in a bar is called *le compte* or *la note*. Confused? It's easier if you just make a scribbling motion with your fingers on the palm of your hand.

A *menu* is a fixed-price meal, not that piece of paper listing the food items. If you want what we consider a menu, you need to ask for *la carte*. The menu is almost always posted on the front of the restaurant so you know what you're getting into, both foodwise and pricewise, before you enter. See "Tipping" section above for tip suggestions.

Lunch is served from around 1pm and dinner from around 9pm. Make reservations!

The French really love their dogs. In restaurants, it's not uncommon to find several dogs under tables, or even on their own chairs.

ESSENTIAL FRENCH PHRASES
please, *s'il vous plait* (seel voo play)
thank you, *merci* (mair see)
yes, *oui* (wee)
no, *non* (nohn)
good morning, *bonjour* (bohn jhoor)

good afternoon, *bonjour* (bohn jhoor)
good evening, *bonsoir* (bohn swahr)
goodbye, *au revoir* (o ruh vwahr)
sorry/excuse me, *pardon* (pahr-dohn)
You are welcome, *de rien* (duh ree ehn)
Do you speak English?, *parlez-vous anglais?* (par lay voo ahn glay)
I don't speak French, *je ne parle pas français* (jhuh ne parl pah frahn say)
I don't understand, *je ne comprends pas* (jhuh ne kohm prahn pas)
I'd like a table, *je voudrais une table* (zhuh voo dray ewn tabl)
I'd like to reserve a table, *je voudrais réserver une table* (zhuh voo dray rayzehrvay ewn tabl)
for one, *pour un* (poor oon),two, *deux* (duh), *trois* (twah)(3), *quatre* (kaht-ruh) (4) ,*cinq* (sank) (5), *six* (cease) (6), *sept* (set) (7), *huit* (wheat) (8), *neuf* (nerf) (9), *dix* (dease) (10)
waiter/sir, *monsieur* (muh-syuh) – note: never *garçon!*
waitress/miss, *mademoiselle* (mad mwa zel)
knife, *couteau* (koo toe)
spoon, *cuillère* (kwee air)
fork, *fourchette* (four shet)
menu, *la carte* (la cart) (this is not an American-style menu!)
wine list, *la carte des vins* (la cart day van)
no smoking, *défense de fumer* (day fahns de fu may)
toilets, *les toilettes* (lay twa lets)

closed, *fermé* (fehr-may)
open, *ouvert* (oo-vehr)
today, *aujourd'hui* (o zhoor dwee)
tomorrow, *demain* (duh mehn)
tonight, *ce soir* (suh swahr)
Monday, *lundi* (luhn dee)
Tuesday, *mardi* (mahr dee)
Wednesday, *mercredi* (mair kruh dee)

Thursday, *jeudi* (jheu dee)
Friday, *vendredi* (vawn druh dee)
Saturday, *samedi* (sahm dee)
Sunday, *dimanche* (dee mahnsh)

here, *ici* (ee-see)
there, *là* (la)

what, *quoi* (kwah)
when, *quand* (kahn)
where, *où est* (ooh-eh)
how much, *c'est combien* (say comb bee ehn)
credit cards, *les cartes de crédit* (lay kart duh creh dee)

KNOW WHAT YOU'RE ORDERING!

Provencal Food & Drink Specialties

aïoli/ailloli, garlic mayonnaise

anchoïade, anchovy spread

banon, cheese dipped in eau-de-vie and wrapped in chestnut leaves

boeuf à la gordienne, braised beef dish

cachat, fresh cheese

cavaillon, a fragrant melon from the town of the same name. It looks like a small cantaloupe

champignon de pin, pine mushroom (a wild mushroom)

daube provençal, gravy with capers, garlic and anchovies

escabèche, raw fish marinated in lime juice and herbs/a cold marinated sardine dish

estouffados, almond butter cookies

farigoule or *frigolet*, wild thyme

fromage fort, extremely soft cheese mixed with herbs, salt, pepper and marc

herbes de Provence, mixture of herbs that includes fennel, lavender, marjoram, bay leaf, sage, rosemary and thyme

lapin en paquets, rabbit pieces in a packet of bacon

lavande, lavender. Lavender blossoms are added to dishes such as sorbet de lavande (lavender sorbet)

lou maïs, corn-meal cake

marc, a strong liqueur made from distilling the residue of grapes (similar to Italian *grappa*)

muge, mullet

parme, amberjack

pastis, anise-flavored *aperitif*. This is a Provençal word meaning mixture. It's a summer drink. Common brands are Pastis 51, Pernod, Ricard, Granier, Prado and Henri Bardouin

petits farcis provençaux, stuffed vegetables

picodon, goat's-milk cheese

pissaladière, pizza-like tart with onions, black olives and purée of anchovies and sardines *provençale, à la*, with garlic, onions, herbs and tomatoes ("Provence style")

quartiers d'orange glacés, caramelized orange sections

tapenade, mixture of black olives, olive oil, lemon juice, capers and anchovies (a spread)

tian de Saint-Jacques et légumes provençal, sea scallops on a bed of chopped vegetables

tomates à la provençal, baked tomatoes stuffed with bread crumbs, garlic and parsley

trouchia, an omelet (in most of France, this means trout)

violet de Provence, braid of garlic

Nice/French Riviera Food & Drink Specialties

bohémienne, eggplant and tomato casserole

daube à la niçoise, beef or lamb stew with red wine, tomatoes and onions

farci, a dish of stuffed vegetables

lou peure, goat's milk cheese with coarsely ground pepper

lou piech, stuffed veal dish

niçoise, usually means with tomatoes, anchovies, vinegar and black olives

pan bagnat, large round sandwich filled with olive oil, onions, olives, tomatoes, anchovies and a hard-boiled egg. A specialty on the Côte d'Azur (means "wet bread"). This is a *salade niçoise* sandwich

pissaladière, pizza-like tart with onions, black olives and purée of anchovies and sardines

ratatouille, eggplant casserole

salade niçoise, salad usually with tomatoes, anchovies or tuna, potatoes, vinegar and black olives

socca, crêpe made with chickpea flour

stockfish, spicy fish stew

You'll also find such Italian pasta favorites as *gnocchi* and *ravioli* on many menus.

Index

PHOTO CREDITS

The following images are from flickr.com unless otherwise noted: front cover: Zoilo Andrés; back cover and p. 7: myhsu; p. 1: Guy MOLL; pp. 12, 165: jean-louis zimmermann p. 17: Olga Khomitsevich; p. 19: Groume; p. 21: Karen Bryan; p. 26: Jean-Pierre Dalbéra; p. 34: Max Froumentin; p. 35: wit; p. 37: klndonnelly; p. 42: Mark McElroy; p. 47: Ming-yen Hsu; p. 51: Gary Bembridge; p.54: Mark Fischer; p. 56: Axel Naud; p. 58: Daniel7omi; p. 59: rdavout from wikimedia; p. 61: Spencer Wright; p. 63: Shruti Muralidhar; p. 67: Tobias von der Haar; p. 70: Yoshi5000; p. 74: Olga Khomitsevich; p. 78: Ivan Matthieu; p. 84: Phil Richards; p. 87: Graham Campbell; p. 92: Ruben Holthuijsen; p. 93: Herman Pijpers; p. 98: Patrick Gaudin; p. 102: Tony Bowden; p. 106: photos/alcn; p. 110: Joshua Morley; p. 111: J.Elliott; p. 113: Elias Gayles; p. 117: Rsuessrb (from wikimedia); p. 118: dierk schaefer; p. 122: Jérôme Ubassy; p. 123: Jialiang Gao (from wikimedia); p. 127: François de Dijon; p. 128: www.rodjonesphotography.co.uk (from wikimedia); p. 130: EmDee (from wikipedia); p. 131: Mike Slone; p. 132: HiP 1; p. 135: Michel wal (from wikimedia); p. 139: decar66; p. 140: Ben Bowes; p. 141: Andrea Schaffer; p. 144: Ernmuhl (from wikimedia); p. 149: Bernard Gaillot; p. 150: Ming-yen Hsu; p. 153: Wolfgang Staudt; p. 154: Claude Valette; p. 161: Yuan Hsueh; p. 166: decar66; p. 170: Ophelia photos; p. 175: dawed bonz; p. 178: ADT 04; p. 179: Elias Gayles; p. 193: Michael Schmalenstroer; p. 199: Michael Gwyther-Jones.

VISIT www.openroadguides.com **for all our travel guides!** Check out two of our newest guides below, also by author Andy Herbach, all about wining and dining in France and Italy. Both are available from amazon.com and other online retailers at a nice discount!

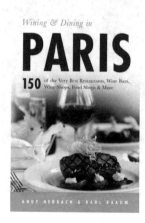

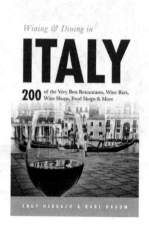